ANTITRUST POLICY
Economics and Law

ANTITRUST POLICY

Economics and Law

Edited with Introductions by
SYLVESTER E. BERKI
CORNELL UNIVERSITY

D. C. HEATH AND COMPANY · BOSTON

Library of Congress Catalog Card Number: 66-26028

PRINTED JULY 1966

CONTENTS

I. WORKABLE COMPETITION, THE RULE OF REASON AND THE *PER SE* DOCTRINE

S. CHESTERFIELD OPPENHEIM

Federal Antitrust Legislation: Guideposts to a Revised National Antitrust Policy 2

WALTER ADAMS

The "Rule of Reason": Workable Competition or Workable Monopoly? 36

II. POWER, INTENT, AND ILLEGALITY

EUGENE V. ROSTOW

Monopoly under the Sherman Act: Power or Purpose? 55

ALFRED E. KAHN

A Legal and Economic Appraisal of the "New" Sherman and Clayton Acts 88

III. STRUCTURE OR PERFORMANCE?

CARL KAYSEN

Collusion under the Sherman Act 117

RICHARD B. HEFLEBOWER

Economics of Size 125

SUGGESTIONS FOR READING 147

INTRODUCTION

The role of antitrust policy in a free economy has long been debated. Is the Sherman Act "a comprehensive charter of economic liberty aimed at preserving free and unfettered competition as the rule of trade"[1] or is it the manifestation of a "destructive principle . . . in irreconcilable opposition to the premises and principles of operation of the free enterprise system"?[2]

On one point it is relatively easy to bring about consensus among lawyers and economists, whether in Government, business, or the academic community. All agree on the need for an economy of decentralized decision-making as one of the requisites of a political system of pluralistic democracy, quite aside from the desirability of competitive behavior as an instrument of economic efficiency. But agreement is less than unanimous that the maintenance of a free competitive system requires any specific legal mechanism. The spectrum of doubt ranges from those who believe that "the morality of the Sherman Act is anachronistic"[3] and that "Like the Lord, competition may well work in mysterious ways so that prices and their changes alone are an inadequate guide to the operation of the 'unseen hand' "[4] to those whose fears of government power and its exercise overwhelm their professed abhorrence of private monopolies. Professor G. S. Becker's statement is characteristic of the latter position: "It may be preferable not to regulate economic monopolies and to suffer their bad effects, rather than to regulate them and suffer the effects of political imperfections."[5]

[1] Mr. Justice Black in *Northern Pacific Railway Co. v. U.S.*, 356 U.S. 1, at 4 (1958).

[2] Sylvester Petro, "The Growing Threat of Antitrust," *Fortune* (November 1962) p. 128.

[3] T. Levitt, "The Dilemma of Antitrust Aims: Comment," *American Economic Review*, Vol. 42 (1952) p. 895.

[4] J. M. Lishan, "The Cellophane Case and the Cross-elasticity of Demand," *Antitrust Bulletin*, Vol. 4 (1959) p. 598.

[5] G. S. Becker, "Competition and Democracy," *The Journal of Law and Economics*, Vol. 1 (1958) p. 109.

Nevertheless, the great majority of practitioners and analysts are in general agreement on the need for some means of legal mechanism to assure the maintenance of some form of economic competition. As yet there is, however, no shadow of an agreement on either the precise nature of the objectives or on the legal-economic criteria of antitrust policy best suited to achieving them.

Granted that competition is to be maintained, what are the acceptable forms of competition? Should atomistic competition, even where the economies of scale might exist, be the goal, or is the rivalry that may arise among the few giant firms of most of our basic industries a sufficient, or perhaps even superior, objective? Are we interested in competition as a way of life, stressing the role and freedom of each competit*or*, or are we interested in obtaining the performance associated in theory with competit*ion*, the efficient allocation of resources and the implied rates of relative factor returns? Or further, should we attempt to establish and to maintain an acceptable competitive structure, and let performance take care of itself? It is in the struggle to provide answers to these questions that the economist makes his contribution. That contribution, however, is limited by his uncertain knowledge of the functional relations among three determining variables: structure, performance, behavior. Thus, rather than derive policy criteria from elaborate but abstract general models, the antitrust economist is obliged to analyze each case at issue within its particular economic context. Given the lack of commonly accepted policy objectives and the paucity of standards by which to evaluate and to predict business performance, it is easy to sympathize with the pessimistic view, "For fifty-seven years we have been playing guessing games with the Sherman Act. It is kind of fun on winter evenings, but it certainly lacks something as a process for working out the pattern of an economic order."[6] But while some economists and lawyers may have despaired, the current Assistant Attorney General in charge of the Antitrust Division of the U. S. Department of Justice has pungently stated that "one of the main functions of economics is to keep antitrust law from being wholly irrational. . . ."[7]

Economic analysis, however, is only one of the three major components of antitrust activity; formation of legal criteria and of procedures are the others. A viable legal code must be more than anchored in broad social consensus that it is just in principle. It must also be compliable.[8] A requisite of a fair and compliable law is that it be predictable. But predictability is the fruit of established rules. The more precisely defined and comprehensive the rule, the greater its rigidity. Yet the situations

[6] B. W. Lewis, "Discussion," *American Economic Review,* Vol. 38, Supplement (1948) p. 211.

[7] D. F. Turner, "Principles of American Antitrust Law," *International and Comparative Law Quarterly,* Vol. 6, Supplement (1963) p. 1.

[8] K. Brewster, Jr., "Enforceable Competition: Unruly Reason or Reasonable Rules?" *American Economic Review,* Vol. 46, Supplement (1956) p. 482.

to which antitrust laws are relevant are kaleidoscopic in their variety. Moreover, the effects of the contested economic practices are neither invariant nor independent of their structural context. Thus arises one of the great legal controversies of antitrust: the "rule of reason" versus the *per se* rule. It can be argued that Chief Justice White's introduction of the rule of reason into the Sherman Act was merely the application of traditional common sense to a new area of legal activity. It can also be argued, and with some strength as Professor Adams demonstrates in his article, that the blanket application of the rule of reason emasculates the antitrust statutes. It makes the Sherman Act a paper-toothed tiger.

There is little doubt that now the antitrust laws are characterized by ambiguity as well as flexibility.[9] The two characteristics are, however, inseparable: to cure the first, you have to kill the second. The broad scope of the rule of reason, with its vacillating emphasis on the roles of intent, of practices, of economic consequences and of predatory acts, has generated an inevitable atmosphere of uncertainty. In contrast, the *per se* rule is rocklike in its definition and predictability.

One can assume at least two diverging positions on the desirability of fixed rules versus generalized principles. The operating businessman faced with a decision can reasonably insist that he know whether the outcome of his choice will be within or without the prohibition of the laws. Hence the business community, and the legal profession when representing the defendants in antitrust litigation, at times clamor for the merits of predictability, even if coupled with rigidity. (It should be said that some of the calls for predictable rules are really *sub rosa* demands for predictably empty rules.) Yet when others advocate the extension of the domain of the *per se,* the narrower definition of "workable competition" (its economic antithesis), or the setting of legal limits on relative or absolute corporate size, such proposals are quickly denounced because of their undesired rigidity in a demonstrably fluid economic world.

Thus the discussion on what the applicable criteria are and what they should be continues. Its resolution is the slow and often painful process of judicial decisions. In this set of readings we are concerned with exploring three major areas of controversy: competition, power, and performance. In each, differing analyses lead to contrasting interpretations of the criteria on which antitrust policy should be based.

The readings in this collection have been chosen for their cogency, their relevance, and the fact that they have not been reprinted elsewhere. The articles by Oppenheim, Adams, Rostow, and Kahn have been somewhat abridged, that by Oppenheim more so than the others. Discussions of procedural issues have been excised as have been most of the footnotes.

It would be naive to assert that these are the sole major areas of current concern in the field of antitrust policy. Disagreement prevails on other issues, among them the implications of oligopoly structure and the

[9] See A. Director and E. H. Levi, "Law and the Future: Trade Regulation," *Northwestern University Law Review,* Vol. 5 (1956–57) p. 281.

definition of collusion within it (what Professor W. Fellner has called "Competition among the few"[10]) and the role and treatment of mergers. Further, there is of course the perennial interchange on the effectiveness of the laws and of their enforcement. Some, as Dean Rostow, maintain that the history of the Sherman Act "is one of futility and half measures, of gallant attempts, occasional victories, frequent retreats, of false starts and missed opportunities." But this view is by no means universal. Others insist that the Act has been effective, that its effectiveness must be measured not by the successes of reported cases but rather by the cases that did not have to be brought. As Professor G. J. Stigler put it: "The ghost of Senator Sherman is an ex-officio member of the board of directors of every large company."[11]

Whether the objectives of antitrust statutes have been properly interpreted and applied (much less whether they have been actually realized), or whether they need modification in a constantly changing complex industrial society are fascinating questions for lawyers and economists. They are vital questions for every citizen. For what happens in the realm of antitrust policy influences not merely the price a consumer pays for gasoline, but the number of alternatives he faces both as the buyer of products and as the seller of his services. And, ultimately, the nature and extent of antitrust decisions profoundly condition the character and direction of an evolving industrial society.

[10] W. Fellner, *Competition Among the Few,* New York: 1949.

[11] G. J. Stigler, "Monopoly and Oligopoly by Merger," *American Economic Review,* Vol. 40, supplement (1950) p. 32.

PART ONE

WORKABLE COMPETITION, THE RULE OF REASON, AND THE *PER SE* DOCTRINE

INTRODUCTION

In his classic article below Professor Oppenheim calls for the establishment of a Committee on Revision of National Antitrust Policy. It was this suggestion, representative of a wide segment of opinion, that resulted in the formation of The Attorney General's Committee to Study the Antitrust Laws, which Oppenheim co-chaired with the then Assistant Attorney General in charge of the Antitrust Division, S. N. Barnes. Professors Adams, Kahn, and Rostow became prominent members of the Committee which published its *Report* in 1955.

Oppenheim views with apprehension recent developments in antitrust decisions which he sees as continually expanding the applicability of *per se* rules while restricting the domain of the rule of reason. He considers the rule of reason to be the only meaningful guiding principle and would have it made applicable to all situations. Contending that economic society of the last half of the twentieth century is significantly different from that of the 1890's, Oppenheim maintains that concepts of competition relevant then are no longer so. To provide a "modernized approach" to antitrust problems he would mate workable competition to the rule of reason and have the resulting offspring legitimized by statutory revision.

To Professor Adams, on the other hand, workable competition is a "snare and delusion . . . a cornucopia of escape hatches," an empty concept totally inadequate as a guide since it "fails to indicate how *much* competition is required to satisfy its pragmatic demands." He disagrees with Oppenheim on the undesirability of *per se*, and with the interpretation that its application has been accelerated and expanded. Adams considers the attempt to combine the rule of reason with workable competition as one well designed to emasculate the antitrust laws. Unlike Oppenheim, and much like Kaysen (pp. 117–25 below) he would emphasize the functional relation between structure and performance and thus would not rule out drastic structural remedies.

S. CHESTERFIELD OPPENHEIM

Federal Antitrust Legislation: Guideposts to a Revised National Antitrust Policy*

I. Re-examination and Appraisal of Antitrust Policy Urgently Needed

A. INTRODUCTION

THE foundation stone in the trio of principal antitrust statutes is the Sherman Act of 1890. Section 5 of the Federal Trade Commission Act and the Clayton Act of 1914, as amended, are the other two members of this major group of antimonopoly laws. While differing in particulars in its impact upon the American economy, each of these basic statutes is avowedly designed to maintain competition in American interstate and foreign commerce.

The antitrust laws in their totality cover a wider area, however, than these three major statutes. Out of the congressional law-making

* From S. C. Oppenheim, "Federal Antitrust Legislation: Guideposts to a Revised National Antitrust Policy," *Michigan Law Review*, No. 50, (1952), pp. 1139–1244. Reprinted by permission of the *Michigan Law Review*.

process in the sixty-two year period since the Sherman Act was adopted has come a surrounding cluster of antitrust enactments of narrower scope. These include specific antitrust provisions in special federal regulatory laws covering segments of the economy, as well as separate statutes and clauses providing various exemptions from the operation of the federal antitrust laws. The pattern of the totality of these laws, as set forth in a recent compilation of congressional action in this field, covers a broad diversity of subject matter and provides a complex system of vesting enforcement authority in various agencies of the federal government. Inevitably, proposals for amendments and supplements to some of these antitrust statutes have been made periodically since the genesis of the Sherman Act.

This area of public law has substantial direct and indirect impact upon the operation of the economy of the nation. Yet growing uncertainty as to just where the federal government is headed in its administration and enforcement of this mass of antitrust laws is casting the shadow of an enormous question mark over many important business decisions which are made today. . . .

The congressional statutory structure of antitrust has produced interacting views in criticism of its inconsistencies and compromises. Some of the statutory provisions "soften" the "hard" competition of other statutory provisions. Exemptions of private interests in some areas, based on political as well as economic considerations, are contrasted with a discriminatory strengthening of the antitrust sanctions against private interests in other areas. Debate also continues regarding the procedures and remedies of federal antitrust laws. Finally, the overlapping in jurisdiction of federal antitrust agencies, highlighted especially by the overlaps in jurisdiction of the Department of Justice and the Federal Trade Commission, has generated demands for congressional action to centralize antitrust administration and enforcement in one source of authority or, at least, to coordinate through a central agency the concurrent jurisdictions of the several federal agencies.

Within the recent past, the critical literature on antitrust has brought to the exploding point pressures pushing toward a complete re-examination of this field of national public policy. Among the significant questions being raised are these:

Are the congressional policies embodied in these laws intrinsically sound in approach? Have the laws been drafted with skill in clearly expressing the objectives, boundaries, and substantiative content of the legislation? Have procedures for both the administration and the enforcement of these laws been wisely conceived and properly executed? Are the separate provisions of these statutes and their relation to one another sufficiently consistent and coordinated to effectuate a unified federal public policy of maintaining competition? What kind, quantum, and quality of competition do these statutes protect? Is it necessary to recast the earlier concepts of competition reflected in interpretations of these laws against newer concepts of "effective" or "workable" competition now widely accepted by economists?

Despite the persistence and the cumulative effect of these widespread questions concerning the existing mass of congressional antitrust enactments, revision of these laws in the past has been on a piecemeal basis reflecting the transient political pressure upon the Congress of one group or another concerned about a particular issue. No attempt has yet been made by the Congress to survey the entire field of antitrust law with a view toward comprehensive revision and coordination of these basic laws. Yet the wisdom and, indeed, the irresistible necessity, of such fundamental inquiry into the question of where the country is heading in enforcing the antitrust laws, and what changes are needed in national antitrust policy, appears undeniable.

This article suggests guideposts for such an appraisal. . . .

B. RECOMMENDED STEPS TOWARD REVISION

Committee on Revision of Antitrust Policy

Evaluation of the functioning of the antitrust laws since their inception has convinced me of the pressing need for a comprehensive and impartial study of our national policy in that field. Such a review and analysis, in my opinion, can best be made initially by a Committee on Revision of National Antitrust Policy, organized and financed as a private body. This committee would act in the role of an Amicus of the Congress in laying the foundation for a sound revision and coordination of the antitrust policy of the United States. . . .

Congressional Declaration of National Antitrust Policy

There should be a formulation of a congressional declaration of national antitrust policy as a frame of reference for clarification of the congressional intention concerning the goals of antitrust and the primary means of achieving them. There is ample precedent since 1933 of like declarations of national policy in various leading regulatory statutes. It is ironical that Congress has never attempted to declare a similar overall policy for antitrust. The suggested declaration of policy should contain three constituent elements of prime significance.

At the outset, the declaration should state the distinctive characteristics of the fundamental ideology of private competitive enterprise under American capitalism. This would not be a gesture in meaningless abstractions and generalities. It would select and reduce to orderly statement the chief features defining the meaning and functions of the private enterprise competitive system upon which there has been a persistent general agreement. This in itself would have a clarifying effect by embodying for the first time an express congressional avowal of the public policy of maintaining competition derived from basic American beliefs reflected in the Constitution and supported by common law and statutory traditions of the United States.

Secondly, the declaration should expressly state that the competition which the antitrust laws seek to foster and maintain is Workable Competition. Economists differ on the definition and content of that concept but there is a consensus that the American economy is characterized by imperfect competition of which Workable Competition is one form. A subsequent section of this article treats this topic in detail. Suffice it to say at this point that, in my opinion, Workable Competition is the most promising concept yet evolved by economists by which the realities of competition in particular industries or markets can be translated into working tools of a modernized approach to antitrust enforcement by the administrative agencies and the courts.

Third, the declaration should expressly adopt the Rule of Reason as a master yardstick of interpretation and application of the general standards of the federal antitrust laws. From my point of view, it has long been disturbing to observe the drift away from this approach in the administration and enforcement of national antitrust policy. In its place, there has been increasing resort to the rigid confines of per se violation rules – a delusive certainty through mechanized enforcement at the expense of the flexibility needed to deal with the actualities of imperfect competition and especially the problems of industrial concentration in big business units among both sellers and buyers. In the respects shown later, the Rule of Reason would provide the central artery of a procedural device for considering all relevant legal and economic factors in any given factual situation. Thereby the concept of Workable Competition can be given the substance and reality demanded by the contemporary American economic system.

These three elements of a congressional declaration of national antitrust policy would represent a substantial net gain in closing the currently existing gap between legal and economic concepts of competition and monopoly. Out of that framework of explicit congressional intention can be built bridges for greater reconciliation of conflicting viewpoints. The declaration would be a master map for direction-finding of basic objectives and means out of which may come a more consistent and better coordinated national antitrust policy.

Revision of Basic Antitrust Statutes

It would be the responsibility of the suggested committee to formulate proposals for revision of the basic antitrust statutes in line with the proposed declaration of national antitrust policy.

The next pages outline the extent to which the proposed declaration would consolidate a great deal of common ground on which government and business may meet.

C. SUGGESTED BOUNDARIES OF COMMON GROUND BETWEEN GOVERNMENT AND BUSINESS

In characterizing the controversies on antitrust one writer aptly said: "The public debate shows signs of being disorderly. It needs an agenda, a common language, and a common ground."

The wisdom of this recommendation is evident. In various parts of this article the task of antitrust revision will be suggested with reference to the above three elements. What follows marks out the metes and bounds of the common ground which government and business should recognize and occupy as a springboard for exploration of conflicting issues.

1. It is academic to debate repeal of the major components of the federal antitrust laws. There is general acceptance in public opinion that so long as American private competitive enterprise endures, the people will continue to regard a national antitrust policy as an unexpendable article of faith in a political and economic democracy. This is so regardless of whether that gospel is expressed in terms of maintaining freedom of competition or in terms of condemning monopolistic aggression. Furthermore, this public opinion remains unshaken no matter how competition and monopoly may be defined in popular, or technical legal, economic, or business usage.

2. Despite cynical references to a "cartel" virus that is alleged to be driving many American businessmen to restrictive agreements and a feverish hunger for monopoly power, American business generally joins the public in support of a federal antitrust policy. This is true of businessmen collectively, even though numerous antitrust cases

themselves attest to individual deviations from the essentials of a competitive struggle according to the legal "rules of the game." That is the area in which antitrust policing is obviously needed. Yet, it is not imputing too much to American industrial leadership to say that it has come of age in knowing that it cannot have the cake of competition and eat the competitors too.

3. To say that the public and business generally stand four-square behind the antitrust laws does not mean that there is indifference to the content and effects of that national public policy. Businessmen have made vocal their insistence that the proper function of government in relation to ordinary private business in this sphere should be limited in the following respects with which this writer concurs:

a. Congressional antitrust policy should continue to place major reliance upon negative proscriptions rather than affirmative prescriptions. It should retain the orthodox pattern of a series of "thou shalt nots." These "don'ts" are the hard kernel of governmental intervention that today gives government and businessmen a firm common ground of concurrence in approaches to antitrust.

b. The experience of over 160 years of American competitive enterprise teaches the lesson that the antitrust laws should not try to displace the organic checks and balances of the opposing factors and forces of the economic system upon which we depend to bring into rough balance the private and public interests. Any attempt by government to substitute as a long-range public policy a spurious omniscience of planned controls for the essentially impersonal and automatic processes of competition in private business would invite a mirage of frustrated hopes. The cross-currents of the ramified American economic order issue from economic freedom of private enterprise in deciding what kind and how much of goods and services to produce, and how, to whom, and at what price, to sell and distribute the fruits of technology, invention, and innovation through private risk entrepreneurship for profit. This quintessence of private discretion is the fundamental reason for adhering to the general use of negative prohibitions upon unlawful antitrust conduct rather than a series of positive mandates of lawful competitive conduct.

4. The antitrust prohibitions mentioned in the preceding paragraphs should be couched in terms of general standards of forbidden conduct rather than by specific enumeration of types of outlawed conduct. . . .

5. These general prohibitions should be interpreted by application of the dominant yardstick of the Rule of Reason rather than by resort to administrative and judicial per se violation rules which cur-

rently tend to nullify the standard of reasonableness. . . .

6. There is considerable evidence of widespread recognition of two beliefs regarding the effectiveness of the federal antitrust laws. One is that they have been a potent force in preventing the American industrial system from developing according to a blueprint of a cartel economy like those of other countries which have never had an antitrust policy. The other is the belief, especially since large-scale dramatization of antitrust enforcement began to make itself felt after 1938, that big business throughout the land has made no important managerial policy or decision without conscious consideration of the prohibitions of the antitrust laws.

7. Antitrust has played a creditable role in the remarkable achievements of the American technological and industrial economy, but cannot alone give us the kind of society we cherish. Government and business, and the public generally, nevertheless look to the antitrust symbols as keeping alive the greater probabilities of a wider scope and better kind and quality of competition under antitrust than under any alternative consistent with the set of beliefs of American political and economic democracy.

II. Tug of War Between *Per Se* Violation Doctrine and Rule of Reason

A. A FEW THREADS IN HISTORICAL PERSPECTIVE

The first step taken by Congress in inaugurating its national policy on competition and monopoly was the Sherman Act of 1890. In 1914 the Federal Trade Commission and Clayton Acts supplemented the Sherman Act. The Federal Trade Commission was introduced as an administrative agency endowed with powers of investigation and adjudication. In the Clayton Act, specific forms of transactions were outlawed where certain effects upon competition are shown. In the intervening years, these three basic statutes have been amended in certain respects. . . .

To attain proper perspective, it is necessary first to notice a major distinction in the policy objectives of these laws. The Sherman, Federal Trade Commission, and Clayton Acts comprise a set of principal federal statutes designed to *maintain* competition by insuring that competition will not be eliminated or drastically reduced. These controls correspond to the area generally described as restraints of trade, monopoly, and monopolistic practices. Section 5 of the Federal

Trade Commission Act and the Robinson-Patman Act amendment to section 2 of the Clayton Act are also in some aspects part of a different set of federal statutes designed to *regulate* competition by marking out a plane of competitive rivalry to insure that the quality of competition is not impaired by the practices prohibited by these laws. These controls correspond to the area generally designated as unfair trade practices. Thus, the Federal Trade Commission Act prohibits unfair methods of competition and unfair or deceptive acts and practices and the Robinson-Patman Act proscribes various species of price and service discriminations.

The distinction between these two sets of laws is not a watertight one. They constitute both opposite and complementary phases of the public policy of fostering competition in open markets. The two sets of laws may be applicable separately or concurrently, depending upon the types of business conduct in issue in any particular case. Unfair methods of competition may be used to reinforce forbidden restraints of trade and monopoly. The effects of the unfair methods of competition may be measured by their impact upon the competitive system. In between, there may be a range of permissible business conduct that does not substantially injure or lessen competition and does not result in excessive competition. In this article, only a few of these differentiations and interactions are considered insofar as they are relevant to the strictly antitrust issues. . . .

Throughout these principal antitrust statutes runs a common problem of a tug-of-war between two rival methods of administrative and judicial determination of when the public policy expressed in the particular law has been violated by the course of conduct challenged by the government.

Antitrust reflects the never-ending conflict between the desire for certainty and the desire for flexibility that is as old as the processes of law itself. The desire for certainty motivates businessmen to insist upon explicit guides to what is lawful and what is unlawful in any given course of conduct within the orbit of the antitrust laws. At the same time, government's interest in expeditious enforcement of the antitrust laws similarly tempts it to seek certainty — this time in absolute rules of per se violation. There is, of course, no paradox in the fact that what the businessmen regard as desirable certainty is not that sought by the government in arguing for the desirability of per se violation rules of enforcement.

B. PER SE VIOLATION DOCTRINE

Per se violation means that certain types of conduct or the existence of certain market conditions are in and of themselves declared unlawful.[1] In antitrust proceedings, rules of per se violation permit the government to sustain its burden of proof merely by showing the existence of the particular operative facts to which the legal consequences of the rule automatically attach. The defendant is thereafter foreclosed from adducing evidence to prove other factors by way of affirmative defenses. He can only join issue with the government with respect to the existence of the basic fact which brings the per se violation rule into operation. He cannot show the effects of that fact in the gestalt of its economic context. In the field of restrictive agreements among competitors, the price fixing agreement is the classic example of an operative fact of a per se violation rule. In the field of industrial concentration, the existence of monopoly power is presently the leading instance of another operative fact of illegality per se.

This per se doctrine obviously works mechanically once the fact of the practice or the market condition is proved. From proof of that fact flows a conclusive presumption – a rule of law – that the effects prohibited by the antitrust laws exist. No evidence to the contrary is admissible. From the standpoint of administration and enforcement of the antitrust laws, the per se doctrine offers an inviting escape hatch from the vagaries of a standard of reasonableness. The question remains nevertheless whether these automatic rules of law do not defeat the true objectives of the antitrust legislation.

C. RULE OF REASON

Diametrically opposed to the per se illegality approach is the Rule of Reason. Against the demand for certainty is counterpoised the desire for the comprehensive coverage and flexibility allowed by application of the general standards of antitrust to specific factual situations through the utilization of a standard of reasonableness.

The Rule of Reason draws the line between zones of legal and illegal conduct under the antitrust laws by consideration of all the

[1] For application of the per se violation doctrine, see United States v. Trenton Potteries, 273 U.S. 392; United States v. Socony-Vacuum Oil Co. (1940) . . . United States v. Aluminum Co. of America, (2d Cir. 1945) 148 F. (2d) 416; American Tobacco Co. v. United States, 328 U.S. 781 (1946); United States v. Paramount Pictures, 334 U.S. 131 (1948). . . .

factors and circumstances in any given situation.[2] It permits consideration and analysis of any transaction or market condition in the light of all the record evidence admitted for its materiality, relevancy, and probative value in relation to the antitrust issues in the case. Whereas a per se rule immediately brands the operative fact embraced by it as unreasonable, the Rule of Reason opens the way to reliance upon a broad range of discretion in weighing the evidence of defenses of justification compatible with the purposes of the antitrust statutes. The Rule of Reason operates through a process of inclusion and exclusion in a case-by-case consideration of all the facts. The per se illegality doctrine operates by converting predetermined single-fact categories into fixed rules of law.

This dichotomy of antitrust doctrine came about as a result of judicial interpretations of the general standards which are present in most of the provisions of the three principal federal antitrust laws. . . . How this see-sawing process of statutory construction explains the emergence of the conflicting per se violation and Rule of Reason approaches to antitrust will now be examined.

D. GENERALITY OF STANDARDS IN PRINCIPAL ANTITRUST LAWS

In the Sherman Act of 1890, Congress chose to use general standards of prohibition. Section 1 of the act declares illegal *every* contract or combination in the form of a trust or otherwise, or conspiracy in restraint of interstate and foreign commerce. Section 3 does likewise for the kinds of commerce more specifically mentioned therein.

The legal pitfall was in the stifling word "every." For twenty years it produced conflicting judicial interpretations until the Rule of Reason dicta in the *Standard Oil* and *Tobacco* opinions of 1911 imported into the sweeping language of the statute the limitation that violations must have resulted from "undue" or "unreasonable" restrictions of competition. This was the genesis of the Rule of Reason, but not its final acceptance.

Section 2 of the Sherman Act contains similar generality of legislative standards. Once again a choice is offered between interpreting the sweeping language of the section inside the rigid framework of a per se violation approach or within the broad and flexible

[2] See United States v. Columbia Steel Co., 334 U.S. 495 (1948); Appalachian Coals, Inc. v. United States, 288 U.S. 344 (1933); Standard Oil Co. (Indiana) v. United States, 283 U.S. 163 (1931); United States v. United States Steel Corp., 251 U.S. 417 (1920). . . .

approach of Rule of Reason tests. The choice must be made whenever judicial meaning is to be given such concepts as monopoly power, monopolizing, or attempts to monopolize any part of the interstate and foreign commerce of the United States. . . .

When the Federal Trade Commission Act was passed in 1914, Congress again adhered to the formulation of general standards by using the words "unfair methods of competition." These are now interpreted by the courts to embrace Sherman Act violations so that their judicial construction coalesces at many points with the trends in judicial interpretation of that basic antitrust statute.

In the various sections of the Clayton Act, Congress in the same manner adhered to general standards so far as proof of effects on competition of the transactions covered in the Clayton Act is concerned. As will be shown later, the Robinson-Patman Act standards do not entirely fit this pattern. With that exception, and the further qualification that the Clayton Act specifies by description the practices it is intended to reach, Congress adhered to the course of formulating its antitrust prohibitions in legislative standards phrased in general terms.

E. DILUTION OF RULE OF REASON APPROACH

If Congress had explicitly adopted the Rule of Reason in each of these three basic antitrust statutes, it would have provided the guiding unifying standard that would have foreclosed the evolution of the queer hybrid of inelastic per se violation rules for some aspects of antitrust enforcement and Rule of Reason flexibility for others that characterizes enforcement at the present time.

These opposing approaches in federal antitrust statutory interpretations have had an impact upon judicial decisions at every level of the American economy. In the scope of application of each of these two trends in judicial interpretations, there is a significant differentiation in two fields. One relates to restrictive agreements among competitors confederated in loose forms of arrangement for joint action, discussed below. Such practices are commonly designated as "cartel" agreements. The other concerns the knotty public policy issues of concentration of economic power through industrial mergers, internal growth, including vertical and conglomerate integration, and other forms of expansion of a business enterprise. This is now popularly known as the problem of Bigness or "Giantism."

With respect to restrictive agreements among competitors, the pendulum of judicial interpretations of the three principal federal antitrust statutes has swung between the extremes of per se violation rules and the Rule of Reason.[3] As of 1952, the trend is decidedly toward application of per se illegality in this segment of antitrust practices.

Historically, the impetus to per se violation doctrine came from the celebrated opinion of Judge Taft in the *Addyston Pipe & Steel Company* case. He concluded that the Rule of Reason was applied at common law only to covenants in restraint of trade which were ancillary to the main purpose of a lawful contract and "necessary to protect the covenantee in the enjoyment of the legitimate fruits of the contract, or to protect him against the dangers of an unjust use of those fruits by the other party." A naked restrictive agreement among competitors was considered barren of such a main lawful purpose since its sole purpose is "to avoid the competition which it has always been the policy of the common law to foster."

In 1927, the *Trenton Potteries* decision was regarded as crystallizing the per se violation rule in price fixing cases. Thereafter, the *Socony Vacuum* opinion of Justice Douglas in 1940 reaffirmed the *Trenton Potteries* rationale and announced many dicta that included in their prohibitions numerous indirect means of tampering with the price structure through joint actions of competitors. A year later, the Supreme Court condemned group boycotts by associations of competitors having the avowed purpose of ending widespread piracy of dress designs and millinery styles.[4] By 1952, the Supreme Court had repeatedly restated the proposition that price fixing agreements and group refusals to deal are illegal per se and, in the *National Lead* and *Timken* cases, the Court applied the same doctrine to foreign commerce agreements among competitors to divide world-wide markets. The Department of Justice has consistently maintained that similar agreements with restrictions on production, allocations of customers, and the like are likewise within the ban of the per se violation rules. Tying clauses and requirements contracts under section 3 of the Clayton Act and certain practices under the Robinson-Patman Act have also been placed in virtual per se violation categories by judicial decisions mentioned in other parts of this article.

There is little doubt that there has been a marked increase in

[3] For differing views on these two doctrines, see: Timken Roller Bearing Co. v. United States, 341 U.S. 593 (1951); Standard Oil Co. of California v. United States, 337 U.S. 293 (1949); Apex Hosiery Co. v. Leader, 310 U.S. 469 (1940).

[4] Fashion Originators' Guild of America v. Federal Trade Commission, 312 U.S. 457, 61 S.Ct. 703 (1941).

the area of applicability of the per se illegality doctrine, especially since 1940, with corresponding attenuation of the Rule of Reason so far as these restrictive agreements are concerned. Indeed, the Antitrust Division of the Department of Justice and the Federal Trade Commission are alert to prevent any infusion of vitality into the earlier decisions where the Rule of Reason was given the Supreme Court's blessing as applied to price fixing arrangements.

The steady advance of the per se violation doctrine, if continued, threatens to dilute the Rule of Reason to the point where it will be so limited in scope as to apply only in exceptional cases. This erosion of the Rule of Reason achieves expeditious enforcement of the antitrust laws through a mechanization of per se violation rules at the expense of the benefits to the competitive system as a whole that are preserved by an assumption of the more arduous burdens of the "Rule of Reason" approach. While there are still areas in which the Rule of Reason is applied, there is an unmistakable danger that the process of attrition, if unchecked, will eventually nullify this standard of reasonableness and reduce the Rule of Reason to a ghostly hue without corporeal substance.

F. CONGRESS SHOULD EXPRESSLY ADOPT RULE OF REASON APPROACH

. . . Whatever position one may take in this controversy, the fact remains that the last word thus far has rested with the courts. The courts necessarily have the final say about the meaning of words in the Sherman Act that are too general to be considered plain in meaning. Congress can intervene in the controversy, however, by providing clearer guides for the courts to follow in interpreting this general language. Thus, a paramount public policy question is whether Congress should now make a deliberate choice by express adoption of the Rule of Reason for application to these restrictive agreements. The effect of this congressional choice would be a repudiation of the present trend toward entrenchment in the law and in the administrative process of the per se violation rules.

In thinking about the consequences of an erosion of the Rule of Reason, there are certain first principles of Anglo-American jurisprudence which should be kept in mind. . . .

Of paramount importance is the preservation of a defendant's constitutional right to a fair and full hearing on questions of fact on discordant issues of antitrust policy. A sine qua non of this right is the proper apportionment of the burden of proof. On the issue of the facts of violation, the government has the burden of proof in its authentic sense of the burden of establishing the existence of such violation. In an antitrust civil proceeding instituted by the Department of Justice, this requires a preponderance of evidence, whereas in Federal Trade Commission proceedings, the applicable standard of proof is substantial evidence shown by the whole record.

The respondent's view of whether he has been accorded due justice in an antitrust proceeding is guided by the traditional concept of his right to have a full day in court. To him this is the indispensable element of procedural due process. Fairness of the hearing given to the respondent on questions of fact is linked with fullness of the hearing. Both are deemed minimal to the rudimentary requirements of fair play.

Applied to the realm of possible defenses to charges of antitrust violation, the per se violation doctrine is repugnant to these fundamental constitutional safeguards. It selects a particular fact – the restrictive agreement or, in industrial concentration cases, a particular market condition – as the decisive fact from which an irrebuttable presumption of antitrust illegality is derived as an immutable rule of law. This at once forecloses a respondent from introducing evidence on the panoply of possible legal and economic justifications in harmony with an overriding public interest of which the antitrust laws may properly take cognizance.

Only the Rule of Reason provides relief from this impasse. Postponing, until later, consideration of the application of the Rule of Reason to industrial concentration issues, let us here analyze the nature of the process and the manner in which it would operate with respect to the apportionment of the burden of proof regarding issues pertinent to restrictive joint conduct of competitors.

It should be recognized at the outset that a congressional code of specified types of lawful and unlawful conduct under the antitrust laws would be only a snare and a delusion. Congress therefore chose the right course when it embodied general standards in the greater part of the principal antitrust statutes. The introduction through administrative and judicial interpretations of per se specific violation rules in displacement of the general legislative standard is equally illusory, if not a distortion of the existing congressional intention.

G. PROPOSAL FOR PRIMA FACIE CASE OF ILLEGALITY

Once this is accepted as a common ground of belief for government and business, the road to a realistic accommodation of the public interest in effective antitrust enforcement and the private interest in conservation of the constitutional safeguards of a fair and full hearing on questions of fact is clearly marked out. . . . For the areas of antitrust law where the per se violation approach has been most pronounced – in price fixing and other restrictive agreements among competitors under the Sherman Act and section 5 of the Federal Trade Commission Act – a prima facie case of illegality should be substituted for the rigidity of the per se doctrine.[5]

In any given civil antitrust proceeding, the initial burden of the government is to introduce evidence of the fact of violation. Upon the government throughout the litigation is fixed the burden of establishing the antitrust violation either by the weight of the evidence, or in Federal Trade Commission proceedings, by substantial evidence in the light of the whole record. This is the true burden of proof in the sense of the assumption of the risk of non-persuasion concerning the existence of the violation.

Substitution of a prima facie case of illegality for the present per se violation rule in the field of restrictive agreements fully preserves this true burden of proof. In accordance with traditional rules, the respondent should have the burden of proof as to any affirmative defenses, again in the real sense of assuming the risk of non-persuasion. When the government reaches the evidentiary stage of showing the existence of a restrictive agreement alleged to be in violation of the antitrust laws, it would be regarded as having established thereby a prima facie case of violation of the statute. Under the per se violation approach, such proof by the government automatically establishes the fact of illegality. Under the suggested prima facie case, however, the respondent at this point would no longer be foreclosed from proceeding to prove other factors in the way of an affirmative defense. Instead, he would then have the burden of proceeding with rebuttal evidence to show justification within the allowable limits of the antitrust statutory standards. If he fails to make such showing, the government will then have adequately made its showing of illegality.

The burden of going forward with the evidence would shift as the trial of issues of fact in such cases proceeds, requiring either the government or the respondent, as the case may be, to come forward with evidence. When all of the evidence is introduced, the trier of fact would then apply the Rule of Reason to the entire record. He would exercise discretion in evaluation of this evidence to arrive at

[5] This is also recommended for tying clauses under section 3 of the Clayton Act.

a value judgment guided by the standard of proof applicable to government and to the respondent. Throughout the whole course of the proceeding, then, the respondent would have a full opportunity to present all the relevant facts he can muster to justify, as an affirmative defense, the merits of his course of conduct. He would, in short, have a full day in court with the knowledge that the trier of fact would give due weight to his side of the controversy. This prima facie case approach appears far more in harmony with due process of law than the present reliance upon per se violation rules in proceedings involving restrictive agreements among competitors.

There is one aspect of the foregoing suggested process of proof which requires special mention. One of the general propositions of this writer's credo is rejection of the blueprint of cartel-like agreements among competitors which, as one writer has put it, substitutes an order of peace for the order of competitive struggle that American national antitrust policy seeks to maintain. There should be no misunderstanding of the writer's antitrust philosophy on this score. There is no intention, in making this proposal, to give aid to any mechanisms fostering erosion of the basic concept of Workable Competition to which reference has heretofore been made. The writer's plea for a full-scale application of the Rule of Reason in the types of situations here under discussion is not to be taken as an invitation to return to the roseate hues of industrial self-regulation through joint agreements among trade association members or other groups of competitors as advocated in the 1920's and as they flourished in the NRA Codes of Fair Competition during the brief life of the National Industrial Recovery Act.

For want of a better shorthand expression than the one which has widespread usage, American antitrust policy has properly been characterized as an anti-cartel policy. The policy itself should remain unimpaired, but without the semantic enslavement of a catchword like "cartel," which may prove to be a tyrannous label misdescriptive of the actualities of a particular arrangement or agreement.

One way of giving assurance that the Rule of Reason would not be misused to give judicial countenance to subterfuge and evasion of the salutary antitrust prohibitions upon unreasonable restrictions upon competition through joint action of competitors is to place upon the defendant the burden of proving by clear and convincing evidence the legal justifications set up in his affirmative defense. This standard of proof may well be for this purpose a desirable alternative to the less strict standard of the preponderance or weight of the evidence and is one which is sometimes applied in common law and statutory standards of proof. In particular factual situations, evidence of legal, economic, and social justifications can then be weighed under close judicial scrutiny to arrive at a determination of whether the restrictions are reasonable or unreasonable when measured against the effects upon competition. Neither government nor business should object to this realistic adjustment between the rigidity of per se illegality and the uncertainty of the Rule of Reason. There would be no weakening of the enforcement of the federal antitrust laws since the standard of clear and convincing evidence would serve notice that exceptions to independent actions of competitors will have a limited range of tolerance in individualized situations where there are overriding legal, economic and social justifications for the restrictions of joint conduct.

H. AGENCIES OF GOVERNMENT SHOULD BE EQUIPPED FOR RULE OF REASON RESPONSIBILITIES

It is not a convincing refutation of the views just stated to contend that the antitrust enforcement agencies of the federal government are not equipped to cope with the burdens that will be imposed upon them by opening Pandora's box of perplexities incident to a thoroughgoing application of the elastic Rule of Reason. American antitrust policy will never come to grips with the inescapable task inherent in the administration and enforcement of the federal antitrust laws so long as either government or business hides its head in the sand to shut out the constantly changing and varied conditions in American industries and markets as they actually exist in structure, behavior, and accomplishments. The relative uncertainty of judicial decisions under the Rule of Reason is a price worth paying for the general standards in antitrust legislation by which flexibility and broad coverage can be achieved. The alternative quest for certainty by blind devotion to per se violation rules produces a rigid formulary system of mechanical rules of law which does violence to the facts of the American economic order. This is too high a price to pay for the government's merely chalking up an impressive record of enforcement successes no matter how hollow those victories may prove to be when they fail to square with the ineradicable facts of industrial life in the United States.

It is disturbing to find that Justice Frankfurter, speaking for a majority of the Supreme Court, has recently given encouragement to the continued dilution, if not the vitiation, of the Rule of Reason by expressions of serious doubts regarding the capacity of the judicial process to measure up to its demands. In his majority opinion in the *Standard of California* case, Justice Frankfurter made certain observations on this subject which are refuted by what the Supreme Court has said and done in other cases in giving meaning and content to the bare words of the federal antitrust laws.

. . . The *Standard of California* decision was based upon illegality attached per se to inferences of prohibited effects on competition drawn from mere proof of the fact of substantially affected commerce. Conjoining his dictum with a misreading of the legislative history of section 3 of the Clayton Act, Justice Frankfurter asserted that a Rule of Reason standard of proof would be "if not virtually impossible to meet, at least most ill-suited for ascertainment by courts." He then supported his conclusion with the following statement appended in a footnote:[6]

> The dual system of enforcement provided for by the Clayton Act must have contemplated standards of proof capable of administration by the courts as well as by the Federal Trade Commission and other designated agencies . . . . Our interpretation of the Act, therefore, should recognize that an appraisal of economic data which might be practicable if only the latter were faced with the task may be quite otherwise for judges unequipped for it either by experience or by the availability of skilled assistance.

If the foregoing comments of the Justice are taken at face value, there would be no scope for the Rule of Reason in any antitrust proceeding where economic data must be evaluated without prior intervention of an administrative agency. This would repudiate any evidence of congressional intention to apply the Rule of Reason in construing the Sherman Act and sections 3 and 7 of the Clayton Act when the case is initiated by the Department of Justice rather than the fact-finding Federal Trade Commission. This effect reached by the *Standard of California* interpretation of section 3 of the Clayton Act has been subsequently reaffirmed in the *Richfield Oil* case. Yet such an escape from the judicial obligation was no more warranted in these latter instances that it would have been in other cases where the Supreme Court has taken a contrary approach.

Without the aid of the intervention of an administrative tribunal like the Federal Trade Commission, the Supreme Court has nevertheless faced up to the task of applying the Rule of Reason whenever it concluded that such was the intention of the Congress. Making allowances for the dissenting views of the justices at differ-

[6] Standard Oil Co. of California v. United States, 337 U.S. 293.

ent periods in judicial interpretations of the federal antitrust laws, Justice Frankfurter's conclusion is diametrically opposed to what the Supreme Court actually said and did in classic instances of Rule of Reason applications in both the field of restrictive agreements among competitors and industrial concentration. Such application of the Rule of Reason is indeed the inescapable judicial task inherent in antitrust so long as there is legal and economic necessity for legislative standards that have "a generality and adaptability comparable to that found to be desirable in constitutional provisions."[7] Justice Frankfurter himself exposed a self-contradictory rationalization of his interpretation of section 3 of the Clayton Act, when he conceded that relevant economic evidence would have been admissible if the Court had found it necessary to decide the issues under the Sherman Act....

Finally, it is especially noteworthy that however much the Supreme Court justices have differed on the scope of application of the Rule of Reason in determining the existence of antitrust violations, the Rule of Reason has been methodically used by the Court in deciding upon remedies to correct antitrust violations found to exist. Surely, in civil antitrust proceedings, this same Court, acting as a Court of Equity, could hardly be said to have a dual-personality, one ill suited to appraising economic evidence when antitrust violation is in issue, the other well suited to such a task when antitrust remedies are in issue. . . .

It is accordingly recommended that the congressional declaration of national antitrust policy, outlined in this article, should incorporate a prima facie case of illegality for restrictive agreements covering any type of joint action among competitors. The Rule of Reason, also to be incorporated in the declaration, should then be made applicable to such horizontal agreements, with the proviso that upon proof by the government of the restrictive agreement, the burden of rebutting the prima facie case of illegality thereby established shall be upon the respondent charged with violation of the antitrust laws. It should be further provided that the defendant shall have the ultimate burden of establishing his affirmative defenses by clear and convincing evidence. . . .

III. Some Trends Toward *Per Se* Violation Approach

In the field of restrictive agreements among competitors, the present tendency to resort to per se violation rules has been fostered by the

[7] Appalachian Coals Inc. v. United States, 288 U.S. 344 at 360.

fallacy of an assumption by the courts that questions of fact and of law can be readily resolved by automatic identification and isolation of the illegal courses of conduct.

In practice, this rule of thumb approach has precipitated a controversy which requires a fresh examination of certain fundamental legal and economic concepts which appear to be lost in the maze of abracadabra.

. . . Only an abbreviated characterization of these trends is presented to reveal the implications of the tug-of-war between the per se illegality and the Rule of Reason doctrines in the controversial zones in question.

A. SPRAWLING NATURE OF IMPLIED CONSPIRACY DOCTRINE

One sector of divergent views concerns the delimitation of the proper scope of application of the implied conspiracy doctrine in civil antitrust proceedings initiated by the Department of Justice and the Federal Trade Commission charging illegal restraints of trade in violation of the Sherman Act.

The concept of conspiracy is of ancient lineage in the law. It is a chief concept under the Sherman Act. In antitrust cases, the Supreme Court has repeatedly stated that no formal agreement and no overt act beyond the act of conspiring is necessary to constitute an unlawful conspiracy under the Sherman Act. It is accordingly plain that an implied conspiracy may be based upon circumstantial evidence of collusive action among competitors achieved through the medium of restrictive agreements. The federal courts and the Federal Trade Commission have broad discretion and great latitude in the reception of such circumstantial evidence.

There has been mounting criticism in recent years of the looseness of the application of this concept of implied conspiracy in antitrust cases. Some writers have vigorously asserted that this tendency has been due primarily to the dicta in the opinions of the courts which went far beyond the ambit of the decisions themselves in their narrow boundaries as precedents on the facts of the particular case.

A storm center of this dispute has been the price conspiracy cases of recent date, especially those which have adjudicated antitrust issues pertinent to the use of the basing point or other types of delivered or geographic pricing.

There is a piece of common ground on which government and business are in fundamental accord. Both agree that proof of conspiracy requires a finding of the fact on an agreement or understanding among competitors to achieve an unlawful end or to use unlawful means prohibited by the antitrust laws. An essential element of this offense is collusive or concerted action. There is no denial that such actual agreement may be proved by circumstantial evidence.

Controversy begins when the line between concerted and independent action needs to be drawn. A series of civil cases instituted by both the Department of Justice and the Federal Trade Commission produced judicial opinions that countenanced in decision or dicta a deep thrust of the implied conspiracy doctrine.[8] The nub of the divergent views of government and business is found in the question of what is reliable circumstantial evidence of probative value in establishing the fact of an agreement. What caused the flare-up of controversy was the extension of proof to inferences of concerted action based upon a common course of action among competitors, each knowing that the others follow the same practice, and a substantial uniformity or identity of result in prices or other elements of market behavior.

Justice Jackson raised his voice in protest against the "loose practice" of applying the conspiracy doctrine, characterized by him as an "elastic, sprawling and pervasive offense."[9] When circumstantial evidence is used in a dragnet or "shotgun" fashion to facilitate proof of an implied conspiracy based largely upon inferences, the disparity between such an inflated legal concept and the businessman's margin of safety in using long established market practices, previously regarded in law and in economics as competitive practices, results in dangling over the heads of businessmen a Damocles sword of antitrust violation.

Once again there is confirmation in this evolution of the implied conspiracy doctrine of the salutary value of the application of the Rule of Reason instead of per se illegality rules. Price fixing conspiracies are but one species of restrictive agreements among competitors. Government has insisted that it is merely attacking collusive action. In the delivered price controversy, the Federal Trade Commission has publicly disclaimed any intention to outlaw geographic pricing as such or to condemn the voluntary absorption of freight by the independent decision of an individual producer who penetrates distant markets to compete for volume of sales.

Out of the morass of arguments and counter-arguments emerges

[8] FTC v. Cement Institute, 333 U.S. 683 (1948) . . . United States v. United States Gypsum Co., 333 U.S. 364 (1948).

[9] Concurring opinion in Krulewitch v. United States, 336 U.S. 445 (1949).

the conclusion that the underlying cause of the disagreement is the government's search for a particular fact or a narrowly circumscribed set of facts from which a per se violation rule can be applied in this implied conspiracy field. This is highlighted by the frequency with which labels have been used as a leverage for the per se illegality approach. "Conscious parallelism of action," "uniformity of conduct," "planned common course of action," "systematic matching of prices," and the like are catch-phrases which at the very least may sometimes inhibit judicial scrutiny of the record evidence to determine whether there is a predetermined or planned actual agreement to fix prices.

Critics who have analyzed the judicial decisions in this area have insisted that the record evidence in many of these cases does not support a finding of conspiracy in the traditional sense of actual concerted action. On this, judgments of appraisal of the evidence may well differ. An important point of agreement is recognition of the hazard that per se illegality rules applied to this field inherently tend toward reliance on a slender reed of positive evidence of conspiracy distilled from inferences drawn from only a few facts. The Rule of Reason would counteract this tendency to set an extremely low minimum of proof of implied conspiracy, especially in cases where the Federal Trade Commission has the latitude of the substantial evidence rule and the advantage of a narrow scope of judicial review of the findings of fact of administrative bodies deemed expert under the law of their creation. Through the Rule of Reason approach, every facet of the evidence would be examined to ascertain both the true nature of the challenged arrangement and its actual or reasonably probable economic effects upon competition in the relevant products and markets in question.

Closely allied to this process of proof is the question of what in fact and in law is a price-fixing agreement. The per se illegality doctrine glosses over this aspect by assuming that price fixing can be readily defined and segregated whenever parallel action of competitors is directed toward any feature of the price structure, as in the case of delivered prices. Price leadership in markets where oligopoly fewness of large sellers and standardized commodities are involved is another phenomenon of business behavior on which viewpoints differ concerning whether price leadership amounts to an implied conspiracy or reflects price competition in imperfect but effective competitive markets.

* * *

IV. Workable Competition: An Approach to Bigness and Monopoly Issues

Another preponderant antitrust area, much more complex and baffling than the subject of restrictive agreements among competitors, is industrial concentration through internal growth of an individual firm, through acquisitions of stock or assets of other firms, and through any mode of horizontal or vertical integration. . . .

The problem of where and how the line can be drawn between legally permissible bigness of industrial units and illicit monopoly is still being thrashed out in the forums and frontiers of legal and economic antitrust concepts. There are many gaps to be filled – gaps between the thinking of those who fear and those who admire Big Business; gaps between those who approve and those who frown upon judicial interpretations which bring large size and monopoly bigness into narrower boundaries of coincidence in applying tests of violation under the general standards of the federal antitrust laws; and gaps in factual data and in the economic tools for measuring the effects of industrial concentration.

A. POINTS OF AGREEMENT AMONG ECONOMISTS

Before dealing with the dominant trends in judicial interpretations in this field, it may be clarifying first to identify the points of general agreement among economists in their reassessment of economic concepts of competition and monopoly as instruments of antitrust public policy.

The common ground developed over more than two past decades consists of the following elements:

Agreement that the polar conceptions of perfect competition and perfect monopoly of neoclassical economics are abstractions that do not reflect the realities of the American industrial structure.

Agreement that between these theoretical extremes there are various forms of imperfect competition in most American industries or markets which should be taken into consideration in weighing the public policy legal issues of antitrust and in resolving questions of fact compatible with the actualities of diversified markets.

Agreement that given varying degrees of imperfect competition in most markets, the task of economics is to formulate standards and devise tools for determining whether competition in realistic harmony with the objectives of the federal antitrust laws exists in specific markets.

B. POINTS OF DISAGREEMENT AMONG ECONOMISTS

The plurality of views of economists and their overlapping make it unsafe to develop further generalizations concerning consensus of opinion about concepts of competition and monopoly. There is, however, recognition of the need for a general re-examination of views in the abridged frame of reference stated above. It may also be helpful to summarize the points of divergence among economists:

Differences in the definition and content of the concept of effective or Workable Competition, which many economists today accept as the guide to national antitrust policy for determining questions as to whether or not in a specific industry or market essentially competitive conditions exist.

Differences in the standards, tests and methods of measuring degrees of industrial concentration deemed compatible or out of line with national antitrust policy in any given species of an imperfect competitive market. From this flow many other points of dissension in viewpoints subsequently discussed.

Most important of all are the differences regarding the economic effects in markets where sellers are few. This is the major sector of disagreement as to how to determine whether Workable Competition, in fact, exists in particular markets. Economic vocabulary now gives currency to the definition of these "oligopoly" markets as those where industrial concentration is manifested in the "Big Three," the "Big Four," the "Big Five" or any fewness of relatively large sellers, who account for the major part of total production and sales, with proportionate power appreciably to influence market price through decreases or increases in output.

Viewpoints interact also on whether American industrial concentration under particular technological conditions must be accepted as inevitable, with resulting reorientation of political and economic values and new approaches to a modernized antitrust policy. A checklist of specific matters on which there is controversy includes problems of the size of the business unit relative to the market structure and absolute size; the relative economy and efficiency of large, medium sized and small firms in different industries; the nature and effectiveness of potential competition with respect to opportunity for entry of new firms into an industry and the presence of adequate substitute products within or between industries; the need for and consequences of dynamic modern technology and its relation to the optimum size of the single plant or multiplant operations, horizontal mergers of companies, and integration on a vertical or conglomerate scale; the significance of strategic resources arising from incorporation and tax laws and issuance of corporate securities, banking and financial connections, technical personnel and research facilities and the like; and the influence of patents, trade-marks, secondary meaning trade names, and similar differential advantages. Many other facets of industrial concentration could be mentioned, but these are sufficiently illustrative to indicate the plurality of cross-currents in contemporary economic thinking about these baffling matters and their meaningfulness for antitrust. There are many federal governmental policies other than antitrust which affect the texture and vitality of the competitive process in American markets.

C. NEED FOR REORIENTATION OF ECONOMIC APPROACH TO ANTITRUST

The core of the resolution of problems of industrial concentration is the widening of the common ground on the kind, the amount, and the quality of competition that can be reasonably expected in the prevalent imperfect markets where elements of competition and elements of differential advantage, characterized as monopolistic, blend in the pattern of the contemporary American industrial structure of private competitive enterprise.

A common obstacle to clear thinking is overstress on semantics of law and economics. This leads to oversimplification and overgeneralization of concepts that have different meanings in different factual situations. . . .

Antitrust lawyers and antitrust economists face a joint task of overcoming the existing barriers to greater coalescence of the judicial and the economic doctrines of antitrust. They are the ones who should provide the guides to clarification of the fundamental antitrust issues of industrial concentration so that by occupation of a wider area of agreement bridges may be built to intelligent exploration of frontier zones where intolerable confusion now exists in both government and business. This need is dramatically brought into focus by the request of the trial judge in the pending *United Shoe Machinery* case for submission of a government brief on the question whether the term "monopoly" is "the equivalent of the economist's definition, or whether it means something else."

In filling the gap that presently exists between legal and economic concepts of competition and monopoly, basic choices must be made from among alternatives in national antitrust policy to resolve as much as possible the endless controversy about the effects of industrial concentration.

D. WORKABLE COMPETITION CONCEPT APPLIED THROUGH RULE OF REASON: A SOUND BASIS OF NATIONAL ANTITRUST POLICY

This writer believes that the main bridge for connecting economic and legal concepts with realistic national antitrust policy should be built on the engineering foundation of the Rule of Reason applied through utilization of the concept of Workable Competition. These are the two synthesizing antitrust concepts previously recommended for incorporation in the proposed congressional declaration of national antitrust policy. Subjective value judgments cannot be avoided no matter what alternatives to this approach may be espoused except by blind reliance on automatic rules of law in the delusive quest for certainty of what is competition and what is monopoly, or what is legal or illegal conduct or market conditions, under the federal antitrust laws. The price of using such mechanistic per se violation rules in the futile hope that they will provide an escape hatch from the inescapable burdens of the Rule of Reason is too high to pay when one considers the unreality of reducing industrial concentration problems to rigid formulae.

E. STANDARDS AND TESTS FOR DETERMINING EXISTENCE OF WORKABLE COMPETITION

National antitrust policy will never find its way toward feasible solutions to problems in the accommodation of the facts of industrial concentration and the preservation of competition in price, quality, and service until it accepts the necessity of weighing all of the salient economic variables in any specific industry or market factual situation. It is undeniable that the Rule of Reason and Workable Competition need the support of a larger reservoir of knowledge and skills than now exists — greater factual knowledge, better instruments of measurements of economic effects to test the validity of assumptions and to determine the probative value of evidence admissible in antitrust proceedings, greater skills of private and government attorneys and economists in legal and economic analysis. In recent years a good beginning has been made in filling this gap. We should press on toward greater progress in that direction.

If Workable Competition in realistic harmony with the federal antitrust laws should be adopted by Congress as the dominant principle for Rule of Reason applications, then it is obvious that in any given situation the broad discretion of government antitrust should be guided by subsidiary standards or tests for determining when

Workable Competition is existent or non-existent.[10] Here, too, controversial aspects need greater reconciliation, but, as is so frequently the case, superficial differences arising from catchword semantics may mask an underlying common ground of understanding of the substance of the public policy issues.

F. INTERACTING VIEWPOINTS OF ECONOMISTS

In a previous article this writer has summarized the opposing contentions among economists.[11] In so doing, two points were emphasized. One is a caveat that any classification of the different approaches taken in the viewpoints of economic thought does not represent sealed-tight compartments, one completely insulated from the other. The other is that economic values cannot be always sharply separated from political and social values of the American democratic system.

Without attempting to repeat here the details of these differentiated approaches analyzed with precision in the compendious literature on the subject, the following is a simplified outline of the main positions on the appropriate economic criteria for testing whether or not the conditions of Workable Competition exist in harmony with the objectives of national antitrust policy:

Some economists *emphasize* the structure of the relevant industry or market.[12] Is it a single-firm monopoly, a duopoly, or an

[10] Blackwell Smith, "Effective Competition: Hypothesis for Modernizing the Antitrust Laws," 26 *N.Y. Univ. L. Rev.* 405 (1951), suggests a statutory amendment specifically providing a procedure under the Rule of Reason whereby certain circumstances would be illustratively specified as relevant to findings of fact on Effective Competition. He mentions the following actual or probable results of conduct, as the increase or decrease of: "(1) Alternatives available to customers or sellers; (2) Volume of production or services; (3) Quality of the services or goods; (4) Number of people benefited; (5) Incentives to entrepreneurs; (6) Efficiency and economy in manufacturing or distribution; (7) The welfare of employees; (8) The tendency to progress in technical development; (9) Prices to customers; (10) Conditions favorable to the public interest in defending the country from aggression; (11) The tendency to conserve the country's natural resources; (12) Benefits to the public interest assuming the relief requested by the government in the proceedings." . . .

[11] Oppenheim, "Economic Background," in a Symposium on Divestiture as a Remedy Under the Federal Antitrust Laws, 19 *Geo. Wash. L. Rev.* (1950).

[12] See such emphasis in following: Blair, "Technology and Size," 38 *Am. Econ Rev.*, Pt. II, 121 (1948); Rostow, "The New Sherman Act: A Positive Instrument of Progress," 14 *Univ. Chi. L. Rev.* 567 (1947); Adams, "Dissolution, Divorcement, Divestiture: The Pyrrhic Victories of Antitrust," 27 *Ind. L. J.* 1 (1951); Levi, "The Antitrust Laws and Monopoly," 14 *Univ. Chi. L. Rev.* 153 (1947).

oligopoly, or is it a decentralized structure with predominantly small business units?

Other economists *emphasize* the actual behavior and accomplishments of the firms in the relevant industry or market in testing the compatibility of economic and legal antitrust conceptions.[13]

In order to avoid imputing dogma to any of these economists, it should again be kept in mind that there is interaction and overlapping of structure, behavior, and accomplishments in any given situation. Any emphasis given to one of these elements becomes a generic difference only when it is in and of itself made the sole test of whether there exists the kind, amount, and quality of competition contemplated by the federal antitrust laws. If such is the case, then the weighing of any one of the three elements is no longer a matter of degree for consideration under a Rule of Reason approach. It then becomes a per se factor upon which a judgment is made according to an inflexible rule of law for dividing the legal from the illegal.

If this distinction is observed, it will furnish the key to an understanding of the dissident subjective judgments of economists in defining the nature and scope of the Workable Competition concept and in making proposals for objective tests of its measurement. When the emphasis on market structure reaches the point where it is contended that the "oligopoly" structure, a crucial one for testing, inherently breeds mechanisms of behavior in violation of the antitrust laws, the rigidity of the assumed causal connection tends to assimilate the "oligopoly" situations to single-firm monopoly situations. The consequence would be that "oligopoly" is thus defined as tacit group monopoly and the conduct of the "oligopolists," in the absence of proof of actual collusion, is branded as equivalent to the abuses associated with restrictive agreements among competitors.

This circumstantial evidence that links oligopoly structure to a conscious parallelism of behavior has the form and content of the extensions of the implied conspiracy doctrine previously discussed. In the process, the accomplishments of the oligopoly industry are given little or no weight at all.

Leaving aside for the moment the single-firm monopoly and duopoly situations, it is fair to say that in the oligopoly situations, the identification of any economic evaluation as a Rule of Reason

[13] See Clark, "Toward a Concept of Workable Competition," 30 *Am. Econ. Rev.* 241 (1940); Mason, "The Current Status of the Monopoly Problem in the United States," 62 *Harv. L. Rev.* 1265 (1949); Mason, "Workable Competition Versus Workable Monopoly," *CCH Symposium on Business Practices Under Federal Antitrust Laws* 67 (1951).

approach necessarily depends upon whether there is genuine willingness to consider all of the relevant economic factors bearing upon the interaction of structure, behavior, and accomplishments in the particular case. This is the approach to which this writer subscribes in company with other writers who have advocated that approach. As previously stated, it is not claimed that the subsidiary economic standards and tests for a sound application of the Rule of Reason have been fully crystallized, although there is encouraging agreement on many of the formulations of these economic fundamentals. Increasing this common ground will initially depend upon bringing together more of the threads of common thinking that in the oligopoly industries no one of the three elements – structure, behavior, and accomplishments – should be made the sole basis for determining questions of antitrust law and economic fact. It would aid in dissipating misunderstanding to introduce into the vocabulary of antitrust the term "interactionists," defined to mean those who, like this writer, believe that the Rule of Reason applied to Workable Competition tests contemplates that structure, behavior, and accomplishments will be each weighed in the context of all of the circumstances of the particular case.

This should go a long way toward lessening the discordant notes in the debates on Big Business or Industrial Giantism. For if anything has shown its head in the public debates, it is on the one hand, the protest from some writers that the government is using an unproved theory of the identity of oligopoly with antitrust violation to reorganize the structure of American concentrated industries[14] and, on the other, the refutations from government sources that government is only seeking to strike at monopoly bigness, sometimes used as synonymous with domination of an industry or excessive concentration. These are merely symptoms of the underlying problem of discovering what is good bigness and what is bad bigness, a distinction which is another way of stating the task set for the Workable Competition approach recommended in the foregoing discussion.

There is no reason why an application of the Rule of Reason to the newer concept of Workable Competition should not take into consideration the teachings of neoclassical economic theories of the price making mechanisms in relation to elements of market structures

[14] See . . . Adelman, "The A & P Case: A Study in Applied Economic Theory," 62 *Q. J. Econ.* 238 (1949); Wright, *Capitalism* (1951); Boulding, "In Defense of Monopoly," 59 *Q. J. Econ.* 524 (1945); Johnston and Stevens, "Monopoly or Monopolization – A Reply to Professor Rostow," 44 *Ill. L. Rev.* 269 (1949).

and behavior. While economists may differ about the importance of the price system as against other market adjustment mechanisms, the preservation of price competition is a vital component of antitrust policy. The real question is what form and degree of price competition can be realistically expected under specified conditions of imperfect competition.

G. TRENDS IN JUDICIAL INTERPRETATION OF MONOPOLY UNDER SECTION 2 OF THE SHERMAN ACT

Turning to the evolution of judicial doctrines, only a sketch of some of the highlights is presented with reference to the extent to which there is a union of legal and economic concepts of competition and monopoly in judicial interpretations of section 2 of the Sherman Act.

In this sector of antitrust, the first milestone in judicial recognition of the application of the Rule of Reason to close-knit combinations was reached in the previously mentioned celebrated dicta of the *Standard Oil* and *American Tobacco* cases of 1911. The sweeping general language of the statute, however, has given the majority and dissenting Justices of the Supreme Court a basis for vacillating between the stifling literalness of a per se violation doctrine and insistence on a distinction between reasonable and unreasonable restrictions of competition arising either from expansion of an individual company or from capital combinations through acquisitions of other firms.

In the industrial concentration field, the Rule of Reason proved to be more difficult for the Supreme Court to resist than in the field of collusive agreements among otherwise independent competitors. Its scope of application has nevertheless been marked by a checkered and uneven course of judicial interpretations. This reflects a variety of factors. The transformation of the American economic system from a predominantly agricultural, local market, and small business organism to a Leviathan of large-scale corporate organizations, with accompanying large-scale technology, and mass production and distribution, is clearly the principal cause of the puzzling antitrust policy issues affecting big business. Shifts in public opinion, the swings of the business cycle, the changing personnel of the Supreme Court, and other factors have also contributed to the ups and downs of the Rule of Reason in this zone of antitrust. Above all, the moving political currents of the American system have come into confluence with changes in the meanings of competition and monopoly as the industrial life of the country progressed to new forms of industry and market structures.

Like section 1 of the Sherman Act, section 2 of the act – the so-called monopoly section – also represents an evolution in the delimitation of its general terms by the gradual process of judicial inclusion and exclusion through the case-by-case process.

In looking back over the entire life of the statute, there has been no single unbroken pattern of tests for ascertaining the boundaries of section 2 violations.

In the early period of interpretation, the percentage share of the market was stressed. In the *United States Steel Corporation* case, the Supreme Court announced the doctrine that mere size is not an offense unless accompanied by abusive practices, but thereafter this was limited by the warnings that size may be magnified to the point of a monopoly and carries with it opportunity for abuse, especially if there has been past proclivity toward such conduct.

As of 1952, the recent section 2 cases have crystallized the doctrine that the indicia of monopolization are the existence of either the power or the intent to exclude competition or to fix prices. If such power is present, a general intent to monopolize is presumed because of the natural and probable consequences of the existence of such power. If monopoly power has not been actually achieved, then a specific intent to acquire monopoly power must be shown.

H. GREATER COALESCENCE OF LEGAL AND ECONOMIC CONCEPTS NEEDED

It is understandable why, in the present state of judicial precedents under section 2 of the Sherman Act, many commentators hesitate to state with precision the extent to which there is a coincidence of judicial and economic antitrust concepts. The decisions and dicta in the *Pullman, Aluminum* and second *American Tobacco* cases together can be explained as achieving such a coalescence applied to a factual situation where a single firm controls all or nearly all of the output of an entire industry with consequent power to fix prices, control production, and exclude potential competition and prevent the marketing of adequate intra-industry and inter-industry substitute products. This is the kind of monopoly power the businessman readily understands, but determining when it exists is another matter.

Economists differ on the tests for determining the existence of such single-firm monopoly power. Some of them stress the importance of first delimiting the relevant product industry and market in any given case as steps preceding an evaluation of the economic effects of dynamic elements in structure, behavior, and accomplishments. Otherwise, they contend, no consideration would be given to the different forms and degrees of economic power which may not amount to the monopoly power condemned by section 2 of the Sherman Act. In the spectrum of this approach are found various shades of distinction. Calculation of the percentage share and resulting extent of power of the alleged single-firm monopolist would depend on the economic boundaries marked out for a product, industry, or a market relevant to the antitrust issues. Contours within and between industries, product differentiation of heterogeneity, geographic areas of markets, functional distinctions among customers, and other definitional demarcations warn against the oversimplification of a unitary monopoly concept clothed in unrealistic universals of existence of power to fix prices and to exclude competitors.

The same considerations are pertinent to duopoly situations where two firms are alleged to share power to control an entire industry, a market, or a product. On this question there are no conclusive judicial precedents under the Sherman Act. In oligopoly situations, untainted by abuses of power or collusion among the few large firms, there are indications of an emergence of a small area of coalescence of judicial and economic concepts as previously indicated. Much more clarification by the slow-moving case-by-case process of judicial inclusion and exclusion is needed before it can be known whether the federal courts will consider all of the aspects of Workable Competition under a full-blown application of a Rule of Reason in oligopoly cases.

I. CONGRESSIONAL ADOPTION OF WORKABLE COMPETITION CONCEPT NECESSARY

If the credo of this article has validity, it calls for congressional action to avoid the effects of the undue uncertainty and confusion in national antitrust policy resulting from the lack of legislative adoption of the Rule of Reason and the concept of Workable Competition as master guides of an improved approach to industrial concentration problems. We cannot afford to wait until judicial decisions under the federal antitrust laws fully determine whether these same guides will be considered as the intention of Congress under the existing principal antitrust statutes. The wisdom of the recommended congressional action is already demonstrated by the vacillations in interpretations of these provisions during the past sixty-two years of antitrust. Explicit congressional enactment of the suggested declaration of national antitrust policy will itself provide positive unifying principles. It will give greater stimulus to advancement of knowledge, skills, and procedures for equipping government antitrust officials, and attorneys and economists who advise businessmen, with improved tools whereby the public and private interests may be brought into better balance in the administration and enforcement of the federal antitrust laws.

Thus implemented, the broad discretion delegated by Congress in the Rule of Reason and Workable Competition rule need not be feared as an erosion of antitrust administration and enforcement. If government and business cultivate the common ground of fundamental thinking delimited in the introduction of this article, both should invite a much needed mutual respect and confidence in their respective sphere of responsibility without sacrifice or weakening of the basic premises of private competitive enterprise.

Utilization of this coherent approach will increase the probabilities of a strengthened empirical basis of antitrust on all levels – in initiation of proceedings, in informal settlements, in formal proceedings, and in court trials and appellate review where the final judgments are rendered on questions of fact and law in determining whether antitrust violation exists and the equitable remedies for correction of violation.

* * *

XI. Recapitulation of Main Recommended Steps toward Re-examination and Revision of National Antitrust Policy

At this point, it may be useful to recapitulate the main steps I have recommended for re-examination and revision of National Antitrust Policy. This is done merely by cross-reference to the parts of this article where the particular proposal is discussed.

1. Formulation of a Congressional Declaration of National Antitrust Policy, containing:

(*a*) a statement of the distinctive characteristics of the public policy of maintaining a private competitive enterprise system;

(*b*) adoption of the concept of Workable Competition;

(*c*) adoption of the Rule of Reason as master yardstick of interpretation and procedure in applying the general standards of the antitrust laws to specific factual situations.

2. Adoption of prima facie case of illegality for application to restrictive agreements among competitors and to tying clauses under section 3 of the Clayton Act.

3. Retention of the generality of standards in terms of negative prohibitions in the Sherman Act, section 5 of the Federal Trade Commission Act, and sections 3 and 7 of the Clayton Act.

4. Revision of section 2 of the Clayton Act (Robinson-Patman Act) in harmony with national antitrust policy.

5. Express provision for application of the concept of Workable Competition and Rule of Reason to Sherman Act, restraint of trade and monopoly jurisdiction under section 5 of the Federal Trade Commission Act, the revised section 2 of the Clayton Act, and sections 3 and 7 of the Clayton Act.

6. Consideration of ways and means of equipping administrative agencies and the courts for responsibilities under Rule of Reason approach.

7. Re-examination of antitrust exemptions in light of national antitrust policy.

8. Retention of concurrent jurisdiction of Department of Justice and Federal Trade Commission with machinery for coordination to avoid duplication of enforcement activities.

9. Formulation of Federal Trade Commission policy regarding written opinions.

10. Consideration of standards for conforming consent decrees to boundaries of antitrust laws.

11. Creation of Committee on Revision of National Antitrust Policy, including consideration of procedures, remedies, and penalties.

WALTER ADAMS

The "Rule of Reason": Workable Competition or Workable Monopoly?*

Vice is a monster of such frightful mien
That to be hated needs but to be seen,
But seen too oft, familiar with her face
We first endure, then pity, then embrace.
ALEXANDER POPE

As part of the currently fashionable and pervasive revisionism, there have been numerous attempts to formulate a new approach to the monopoly problem. Two of these efforts deserve special attention — the report by the Business Advisory Council of the Secretary of Commerce[1] and the monumental study by Professor S. Chesterfield Oppenheim.[2] They reach strikingly similar conclusions and offer parallel recommendations. Both find that recent judicial interpretation of the antitrust laws has been shifting, vague, confusing, and uncertain; that a unifying standard for judging antitrust violations is imperative; and that such a standard can be achieved through revitalization of the "Rule of Reason" and acceptance of "Workable Competition." Both studies concur in Professor Oppenheim's assurance that "the broad discretion delegated by Congress in the Rule of Reason and Workable Competition rule need not be feared as an erosion of antitrust administration and enforcement." While this may at first

* From Walter Adams, "The Rule cf Reason: Workable Competition or Workable Monopoly?" Reprinted by permission of the copyright holder from *The Yale Law Journal*, Volume 63, Number 3, pp. 348–370. Single issues, as well as back issues available at $2.50 from Fred B. Rothman, 57 Leuning Street, South Hackensack, New Jersey. Subscription, $10.00 per volume available from Business Office, *The Yale Law Journal*, 401-A Yale Station, New Haven, Conn., 06520. Copyright © 1953, by the Yale Law Journal Co. Reprinted also by permission of the author.

[1] Business Advisory Council, *Effective Competition* (1952) (hereinafter cited as Business Advisory Council).

[2] See above, pp. 2–35 [Ed. note].

blush appear to be old wine in new bottles, the new approach represents a significant departure in the antitrust field. Its importance lies in the combination of legal and economic pragmatism into an instrument for attacking the traditional philosophy of antitrust. It is the thesis of this article that the new approach is subject to severe limitations, if not fatal defects; that the interpretation of the Sherman Act is far less uncertain than its critics imply; that a "Rule of Reason," as these critics use the phrase, would mean judicial emasculation of Section 1 of the Act; and finally, that acceptance of what they mean by "Workable Competition" would be tantamount to a toleration of monopoly under Section 2.[3]

Under Section 1 of the Act, the courts have confronted the problem of determining whether or not a given business arrangement involved a restriction of competition which was to be conclusively presumed "unreasonable." Business arrangements which fall into the categories of price fixing, market sharing, or boycotts growing out of joint action among competitors are subject to this conclusive presumption which makes them illegal per se. Some commentators have chosen to regard this per se doctrine as part of, and subsumed under, the rule of reason. They have argued that "per se" does not eliminate the necessity of exercising reasonableness in determining whether or not a given arrangement fits into a forbidden category. Other commentators, however, feel that the per se doctrine and the rule of reason are incompatible; that there is a sharp dichotomy dividing the two; that the per se doctrine forecloses an examination of the reasonableness (economic desirability) of a given business arrangement, whereas a genuine rule of reason should not. Since both Professor Oppenheim and the Business Advisory Council take the latter view of a rule of reason under Section 1, we shall, for purposes of this article, accept their definition.

[3] Although all commentators reject the standard of "pure" or "perfect" competition, there is disagreement as to the nature of the substitute standard — "workable competition." Some view it as giving "equal emphasis on market structure and market behavior." Rostow & Sachs, "Entry into the Oil Refining Business: Vertical Integration Re-examined," 61 *Yale L.J.* 856, 862 (1952). Others emphasize the performance of the defendants in their industry. Mason, "The Current Status of the Monopoly Problem in the United States," 62 *Harv. L. Rev.* 1265, 1281–2 (1949). Oppenheim and the Business Advisory Council adopt the latter view and emphasize the market performance criterion. Although the author agrees with Professor Rostow, we shall, for purposes of this article, be referring to the market performance viewpoint when discussing the "workable competition" advocated by Professor Oppenheim and the Business Advisory Council.

UNCERTAINTY

The Business Advisory Council complains that: "The interpretation and administration of the Antitrust Laws are so lacking in consistent clear standards related to practical performance that no businessman can tell whether or not he is conforming with or violating the spirit and intent of the various statutes. The businessman's lawyer cannot give reliable guidance." In endorsing this view, Professor Oppenheim states that "growing uncertainty as to just where the federal government is headed in its administration and enforcement of this mass of antitrust laws is casting the shadow of an enormous question mark over many important business decisions which are made today." It is this charge of uncertainty which is then made the basis of demands for legislative revisions. The extent to which the charge is justified depends on the extent to which the law is, in fact, uncertain.

With respect to price fixing agreements, judicial interpretation of Section 1 has remained surprisingly constant over the years. In the *Addyston Pipe & Steel* case, Judge Taft refused to examine the reasonableness of the agreement; he refused to "set sail on a sea of doubt" and to assume the power of saying "how much restraint of competition is in the public interest, and how much is not." He wisely observed that "the manifest danger in the administration of justice according to so shifting, vague, and indeterminate a standard would seem to be a strong reason against adopting it." And, in *Standard Oil Co. v. United States,* the Supreme Court declared that agreements, if "clearly restraints of trade within the purview of the statute, . . . could not be taken out of that category by indulging in general reasoning as to the expediency or non-expediency of having made the contracts or the wisdom or want of wisdom of the statute which prohibited their being made." Here was the nucleus of the per se doctrine to which the Business Advisory Council and Professor Oppenheim take unqualified exception.

This per se doctrine was further crystallized in the *Trenton Potteries* case. There Mr. Justice Stone held that every price fixing agreement, if effective, eliminates one form of competition. He rejected the defense that fixed prices, if reasonable, cause no injury to the public interest. The *ratio decidendi* was unmistakable: the reasonable price of today may become the unreasonable and arbitrary price of tomorrow. Under Oppenheim's rule of reason, and in the absence of competition, enforcement agencies would be compelled to conduct continuous and minute inquiry into the reasonableness of a particular price; they would have to ascertain from day to day whether an initially reasonable price had, through the normal change of economic conditions, become unreasonable. Hence, Justice Stone concluded, "Agreements which create such potential power may well be held to be in themselves unreasonable or unlawful restraints. . . ." He hesitated "to adopt a construction making the difference between legal and illegal conduct in this field of business relations depend upon so uncertain a test as whether prices are reasonable – a determination which can be satisfactorily made only after a complete survey of our economic organization and a choice between rival philosophies."

After a deviation in the *Appalachian Coals* case,[4] the per se doctrine was again applied in the *Socony-Vacuum* case. There Justice Douglas affirmed the *Trenton Potteries* doctrine, and in numerous dicta condemned both abortive and successful, direct and indirect means of tampering with the price structure through joint action among competitors. Price fixing agreements were declared to be unlawful under Section 1 of the Sherman Act regardless of the amount of interstate or foreign commerce involved. "Whatever may have been the status of price-fixing agreements at common law. . . the Sherman Act has a broader application to them than the common law prohibitions or sanctions. . . . Whatever economic justification particular price-fixing agreements may be thought to have, the law does not permit an inquiry into their reasonableness. They are all banned because of their actual or potential threat to the central nervous system of the economy."

Subsequently the per se doctrine was apparently extended to boycotts growing out of joint action by competitors, and to price fixing agreements and market sharing arrangements in foreign commerce. In view of this almost monolithic evolution of the case law under Section 1, it is difficult, if not impossible, to ascertain the respects in which the law is unclear or uncertain. In fact, it could readily be argued that the trouble with Section 1 is not that it is unclear, but that it has become painfully clear, and that the hope of prospective price fixers is not to clarify the trend, but to reverse it.

Experience justifies a less drastic view of the clamor for clarifying Section 2 of the Act. Here there has been considerable judicial vacillation. In the earlier cases under Section 2, the courts tended to follow the rule that "size does not determine guilt; that there must be some 'exclusion' of competitors; that the growth must be something

[4] Appalachian Coals, Inc. v. United States, 288 U.S. 344 (1933). Despite Mr. Justice Douglas' heroic, but unpersuasive, attempt to distinguish rather than overrule the *Appalachian* case in United States v. Socony-Vacuum Oil Co., 310 U.S. 150, 214 (1940), few would regard *Appalachian* as a controlling precedent today. . . .

else than 'natural' or 'normal'; that there must be a 'wrongful intent,' or some other specific intent; or that some 'unduly' coercive means must be used."[5] Since World War II, however, the courts have tended to emphasize the significance of market power, and to infer a general intent to monopolize from a course of conduct directed toward the achievement, retention, or extension of monopoly power.[6] A monopolist was presumed to have engaged in monopolization unless he could show that monopoly "was thrust upon" him. With increasing clarity there has emerged the view that Section 2 does not condone good trusts and condemn bad trusts, but forbids all trusts. Under the "new" Sherman Act,[7] the standard applied in Section 2 cases is not whether prices have actually been raised or competitors actually excluded, but whether power exists, coupled with an intent and purpose, to raise prices and exclude competitors whenever it is desired to do so. It is this test – the so-called market structure test – which is coming into sharper focus and which is now the object of growing criticism. While the test may ultimately be rejected as economically unfeasible or undesirable, it cannot be attacked as legally unclear.

Yet the alleged unclarity and vagueness of the case law is offered as justification for the persistent effort to upset the per se doctrine under Section 1, and the market structure test under Section 2 of the Sherman Act. The remedy suggested both by Professor Oppenheim and the Business Advisory Council is the application of the rule of reason to *both* sections. As the Business Advisory Council put it: "The old Rule of Reason, if applied, would cure part of the problem, if revived, because it is flexible – but it is also highly indefinite. Most businessmen and lawyers, even so, prefer the flexibility of a Rule of

[5] United States v. Aluminum Co. of America, 148 F.2d 416, 429 (2d Cir. 1945). This test was applied in Standard Oil Co. v. United States, 221 U.S. 1 (1911), and in United States v. American Tobacco Co., 221 U.S. 106 (1911); it was affirmed in United States v. U. S. Steel Corp., 251 U.S. 417, 451 (1920); it was ignored in United States v. Reading Co., 253 U.S. 26 (1920); it was reaffirmed in United States v. International Harvester Co., 274 U.S. 693, 708 (1927); and it was diluted in United States v. Swift & Co., 286 U.S. 106, 116 (1932) ("Mere size . . . is not an offense against the Sherman Act unless magnified to the point at which it amounts to a monopoly. . . , but size carries with it an opportunity for abuse that is not to be ignored when the opportunity is proved to have been utilized in the past.").

[6] See, *e.g.*, American Tobacco Co. v. United States, 328 U.S. 781 (1946); United States v. Aluminum Co. of America, 148 F.2d 416 (2d Cir. 1945).

[7] Rostow, "The New Sherman Act: A Positive Instrument of Progress," 14 *U. of Chi. L. Rev.* 567 (1947); Rostow, "Monopoly Under the Sherman Act: Power or Purpose?" [Reprinted here, pp. 00–00.]

Reason, even with its indefiniteness." In a way, this argument lets the cat out of the bag. Its inconsistency with the demands for greater clarity and certainty is so obvious, that it is best treated *sub silentio*.

However, there is another cure for uncertainty which does require comment. The Business Advisory Council suggests that provision be made for advisory opinions ("authoritative rulings") on activities which may be variously construed under diverse interpretations of the antitrust laws. The businessman, it is said, is quite willing to comply with the law if he can find out what to comply with. Hence the Council advocates authoritative rulings as well as special legislation to prevent retroactive impact from any reversal of position by the Government. This procedural change, while it appears innocent and plausible, is both dangerous and unnecessary. Louis D. Brandeis emphasized this rather pointedly when he counseled the newly created Federal Trade Commission not to grant advisory opinions. He argued that it would be impossible for the FTC to determine in advance whether or not the contemplated behavior would result in an improper restraint of trade, and that such a determination would necessitate knowledge of the effect of the contemplated behavior on competitors who would not be available at the advisory hearing.[8]

On the basis of the available evidence, it may not be inappropriate to suggest that interpretation of the Sherman Act is less vague, unclear, and confusing than its critics imply; that if, arguendo, the law's enforcement were indeed vague and shifting, the rule of reason is hardly the appropriate remedy; and finally, that the advisory opinion suffers from defects which may vitiate its utility.

RESTRAINT OF TRADE

With respect to Section 1 violations, Professor Oppenheim objects to the per se doctrine because it selects a particular fact, *e.g.*, price fixing, as establishing an irrebuttable presumption of antitrust violation without permitting the respondent to introduce evidence by way of legal or economic justification for the alleged restraint. Under the Oppenheim proposal, by contrast, the Government would still have the burden of proving a contract, combination, or conspiracy in restraint of trade, but such showing would be no more than a prima facie presumption of unlawful conduct. The respondent would then be allowed to present rebuttal evidence to show economic and legal justifications in "harmony with an overriding public interest." As Professor

[8] Testimony of Louis D. Brandeis, *FTC Records* 2–9 (1915).

Oppenheim puts it: "Throughout the whole course of the proceeding, then, the respondent would have a full opportunity to present all the relevant facts he can muster to justify, as an affirmative defense, the merits of his course of conduct. He would, in short, have a full day in court with the knowledge that the trier of fact would give due weight to his side of the controversy. This prima facie case approach appears far more in harmony with due process of law than the present reliance upon per se violation rules in proceedings involving restrictive agreements among competitors." To prevent misuse of his rule of reason as a cloak for subterfuge and evasion of antitrust prohibitions, Professor Oppenheim would place "upon the defendant the burden of proving by clear and convincing evidence the legal justifications set up in his affirmative defense." Thus, while the Government's case would be judged by the preponderant weight of the evidence, the defendant would have to meet the more exacting burden of clear and convincing evidence. With this safeguard, Professor Oppenheim feels that there is little cause to fear an erosion of effective antitrust enforcement.

It is not unfair to say that this approach would replace our traditional reliance on competition as a regulator of economic affairs. Under the new standard, price fixing might be deemed lawful if the prices fixed were reasonable, *i.e.*, did not injure the public interest. The crucial test would be performance; "good" social ends would justify hitherto anti-social means. Or, to put it in the classic parlance of pragmatic realism: as long as the trains are on time, the method of determining schedules is of secondary importance.

It is significant that nowhere does Professor Oppenheim spell out the types of defenses to be admitted by way of rebutting a prima facie presumption of unlawful conduct. Yet, judging by the justifications offered in previous price fixing cases, we have some notion of what the leading defenses are likely to be. In the past, the affirmative defenses included the contention that (1) the industry is peculiarly vulnerable to ruinous competition; (2) the prices fixed are reasonable; (3) depressed conditions in the industry make a restraint on price competition imperative; and (4) the price fixing arrangement is innocuous since it lacks the power to set prices. An examination of each of these defenses may throw some light on the efficacy of the "new approach."

Ruinous Competition

This defense contends that unrestrained price competition, while generally desirable, is unworkable in the industry in question. Thus, in the *Trans-Missouri* case defendants claimed that "competition while, perhaps, right and proper in other business, simply leads in railroad business to financial ruin and insolvency." In the railroad industry, with its heavy capital investments and decreasing costs per unit, each road must attract additional freight in order to increase revenues. Since other roads are similarly motivated, any price cut will meet with inevitable retaliation – to the detriment of all. "The only refuge, it is said, from this wretched end lies in the power of competing roads agreeing among themselves to keep up prices for transportation to such sums as shall be reasonable in themselves, so that companies may be allowed to save themselves from themselves, and to agree not to attack each other, but to keep up reasonable and living rates for the services performed."

Similar claims have been made for other industries. A former trustee of the Cement Institute, for example, in defending the collusive basing point system, once wrote that cement was an industry "above all others that cannot stand free competition, that must systematically restrain competition or be ruined."[9] These examples can be multiplied. All raise the central issue whether exemptions from the antitrust laws should lie in the discretion of the courts, or in the legislative domain of Congress. Certainly, past experience indicates that Congress has granted exemptions without reluctance wherever it thought that a particular situation or the conditions of a particular industry justified such action. It would seem that in a democracy it is for the elected representatives of the people and not for private groups (subject to judicial veto) to decide whether or not a particular industry is capable of withstanding the rigors of competitive rivalry.

Reasonable Prices

In every price fixing case, there is inevitably offered the defense that the prices fixed are reasonable. This raises the fundamental and difficult problem of selecting a proper standard of reasonableness, *i.e.*, a standard suitable for judicial application. Assuming that a proper standard for judging the reasonableness of prices can be found, it is at best doubtful whether the courts can provide that detailed and continuous supervision over prices which, in the absence of competition, would be imperative. Moreover, it is questionable whether a court should, in effect, be converted into an administrative agency guarding the public against potential exploitation.

The basic policy question is this: shall the businessman be per-

[9] Quoted in FTC v. Cement Institute, 333 U.S. 683, 706 (1948).

mitted to forsake competition and engage in price fixing and other trade restraints while simultaneously avoiding effective regulation in the public interest? Can the public be expected to rely on industry self-government, enlightened stewardship, or benevolent economic despotism as desirable alternatives to a free market? Competition is only one technique of social control; one method for limiting the power of individual firms over the economy. If competition is to be abandoned, an adequate safeguard must be put in its place. The price fixer's fear of potential rebuke by the courts does not appear to be such a safeguard.

Depressed Condition of the Industry

This defense was most forcefully and persuasively presented in the *Appalachian Coals* case of 1933. Given the depressed condition of the coal industry, it was argued that a joint selling agency covering 73 percent of the producers in the Appalachian field was a reasonable restraint of trade. . . .

The coal industry in 1933 was, of course, a classic milieu for the "depressed industry" argument. Yet it is debatable whether, even in this case, the restraint could be justified by sound economic principles. To the extent that coal's afflictions were attributable to the business cycle, the pricing arrangement in question was hardly a suitable remedy. Depressions can be attacked most effectively with countercyclical monetary and fiscal weapons which strike at the root of the difficulty; they cannot be cured by price fixing schemes. Moreover, overexpansion of capacity cannot be undone even by collusive devices. European cartels, for example, have repeatedly tried to eliminate warborn overcapacity only to find that their artificial restraints tended to perpetuate such capacity, and intensify competition from non-members and substitute products.[10] Furthermore, the effort to maintain or raise prices artificially is not likely to arrest the long-run decline of one industry relative to competing industries. To the extent that such price manipulations are successful, they tend to accelerate, not arrest, the decline of a depressed industry. Finally, concentration of power on the buying side of the market does not justify

[10] *See* Stocking & Watkins, *Cartels in Action* c. 3 (1950). Excess capacity, resulting from over-expansion, does not disappear through cartelization. If the cartel allocates the limited demand to its membership through output quotas, or if the cartel attempts to maintain artificial prices (thus curtailing consumption), existing facilities will not be fully used. This unused capacity represents a cost for which someone – in this case, the consumer – has to pay. Here, as in other areas of economic life, "there is no such thing as a free lunch."

the promotion of countervailing power on the selling side. An alternative solution, equally logical and more consistent with the competitive philosophy, would be to dispel the source of original market power. In short, the depressed condition of an industry certainly may call for some remedial action; but it is questionable whether unsupervised private action, involving significant departures from competition, constitutes the most fruitful and least dangerous method of attack.

Lack of Market Power

In the *Appalachian Coals* case defendants argued that only 73 percent of the field's production was covered by the agreement; that Appalachian coal had to compete with that of other regions; that entry into the industry (potential competition) was unfettered; and that defendants' concerted action might incidentally "affect" market price, but could not set it. Similarly, in the *Socony-Vacuum* case, defendants urged that their purchase program for "distress" gasoline had no "effect on the competitive market price beyond that flowing from the removal of a competitive evil; and that if [they] had tried to do more than free competition from the effect of distress gasoline and to *set an arbitrary non-competitive price through their purchases, they would have been without power to do so.*"

Assuming these contentions to be valid, it would still be true that attempts to raise, lower, or stabilize prices through joint action of competitors involve a direct interference and tampering with the free play of market forces. Even though a particular price fixing agreement may fall short of power to control or dominate a given market, it still has an influence on market price and may be of considerable value to the conspirators; else they would not, as rational businessmen, adhere to it. Moreover, even a monopolist lacks power – in any absolute sense – to control market price, because he is limited by the competition of substitute products and the fear of potential competition. Finally, it is to be noted that price fixing is distinct from monopolizing, and that the Sherman Act condemns the former as well as the latter. "The existence or exertion of power to accomplish the desired objective . . . becomes important only in cases where the offense charged is the actual monopolizing of any part of the trade or commerce in violation of § 2 of the Act. . . . An intent and a power to produce the result which the law condemns are then necessary. . . . But the crime under § 1 is legally distinct from that under § 2. . . . Only a confusion between the nature of the offenses under those two sections . . . would lead to the conclusion that power to fix prices was necessary for proof of a price-fixing conspiracy under § 1."[11] In short, the lack of monopoly power is hardly an adequate defense to a charge of price fixing.

* * *

MONOPOLY

With regard to Section 2 violations, Professor Oppenheim observes that current debates over enforcing the law against monopoly bigness are merely symptomatic of "the underlying problem of discovering what is good bigness and what is bad bigness." He decries excessive reliance on the market structure standard under which oligopoly is often regarded as tacit group monopoly, and oligopoly conduct is considered equivalent to restrictive agreements among competitors, in the absence of proof of actual collusion. "In the process, the *accomplishments* of the oligopoly industry are given little or no weight at all."

For this reason both Professor Oppenheim and the Business Advisory Council suggest a new interpretation of Section 2 which would place primary emphasis not on market structure but on market performance.[12] Good monopolies would be distinguished from bad monopolies, hinging the difference between the two on the performance test of workable competition. Despite the statutory language which prohibits all monopolizing, Professor Oppenheim would condemn only those market organizations which are both monopolistic and injurious to the public interest. He apparently adopts the following criteria for judging performance in the public interest: "(1) Alternatives available to customers or sellers; (2) Volume of production or services; (3) Quality of the services or goods; (4) Number of people benefited; (5) Incentives to entrepreneurs; (6) Efficiency and economy in manufacturing or distribution; (7) The welfare of employees; (8) The tendency to progress in technical development; (9) Prices to customers; (10) Conditions favorable to the public interest in defending the country from aggression; (11) The tendency to conserve the country's natural resources; (12) Benefits to the public interest assuming the relief requested by the government in the pro-

[11] United States v. Socony-Vacuum Oil Co., 310 U.S. 150, 226 n. 59 (1940).

[12] While Professor Oppenheim concedes the necessity of weighing "all of the relevant economic factors bearing upon the interaction of structure, behavior, and accomplishments in the particular case," it is apparent that accomplishments (performance) occupy a central and dominant position in his trinity of standards.

ceedings."[13] This approach to the monopoly problem is subject to rather severe limitations.

The Snare and Delusion of Workable Competition

Workable competition overemphasizes the significance of inter-industry, inter-product, and technological competition. The Business Advisory Council, in illustrating the operation of workable competition, observes that aluminum "must compete with steel, copper, zinc, lead, tin, wood, textiles, plastics, paper, clay, glass, leather and cork. . . . Timber, the ancient material, has been rejuvenated through modern chemistry. The textile industry has been revolutionized both by chemistry and by technical machinery. The former transport dominance of the railroad industry has long been lost to highway and air competition. Such examples could be multiplied." To the Council this is proof of workable competition – or what it calls effective competition – in action. This it regards as preferable to the abstract and unrealistic "perfect" competition of classical economic theory as a standard for applied public policy.

Three observations are relevant on this score. First, as Henry Simons has pointed out, "no sane advocate is asking for perfect competition, and no critic who is at once fair and competent will picture the [antitrust] policy as requiring drastic change in the organization of production. The requisite changes have to do mainly with ownership units and control devices, not with operation."[14] Antitrust supporters do not demand that the economy be purified right out of the twentieth century.[15] They do suggest, however, that in most industries competition can be increased without diminution of technological efficiency.

Secondly, inter-industry competition as an economic force is more apparent than real. The fact is that when the paper container posed a threat to the tin can duopoly, Continental Can entered the paper container industry; when magnesium challenged the aluminum monopoly, Alcoa joined the magnesium cartel; when aluminum became a substitute for copper, Anaconda embarked on its venture into the

[13] Smith, "Effective Competition: Hypothesis for Modernizing the Antitrust Laws," 26 *N.Y.U.L.Q. Rev.* 405 (1951), quoted in Oppenheim. While Professor Oppenheim tentatively endorses these standards, he suggests that different standards may be equally acceptable if formulated by the national committee on the antitrust laws proposed in his article.

[14] Simons, *Economic Policy for a Free Society* 82 (1948).

[15] See Kahn, "Standards for Antitrust Policy," 67 *Harv. L. Rev.* 28, 35 (1953).

aluminum industry. Today railroads control bus lines, shipping companies are tied to airlines, newspapers control radio stations, and TV outlets are operated by licensees of AM stations. Most serious, perhaps, is the Government's official blessing of important mergers in the communications industry, such as the recent combination of motion picture and television holdings. Besides being only a limited substitute for intra-industry rivalry, inter-industry competition can be manifestly subverted by control on the highest level of intercorporate finance.

Thirdly, inter-industry competition is perfectly compatible with a fully monopolized economy. Even if the aluminum, copper, steel, and magnesium industries were each a 100 percent monopoly, they could still theoretically compete with each other. Moreover, such competition might well qualify as "effective" under the standards of the Business Advisory Council, for there would still be *"unhampered business incentives and freedom of choice, with reasonable alternatives for buyers and sellers."* The incentives, to be sure, would exist for the few and not the many; the alternatives would be those which the respective monopolists, in their role as industrial stewards, made available to the fortunate beneficiaries of modern technology.

Workable Competition and Effective Antitrust Enforcement

Workable competition tends to obliterate any practical guidelines to effective antitrust enforcement. It fails to indicate *how much* competition is required to satisfy its pragmatic demands. All we are told is that that there must be enough competition to provide reasonable alternatives. "When consumers can choose freely between alternative sellers, each seller has an incentive to improve his product and lower his price. Consumers are thereby protected against monopolistic exploitation."

This is hardly a clear, definite, or measurable standard. Obviously, there will always be some competition and some freedom of choice under almost any form of economic organization. The history of cartels, for example, is replete with instances where cartel policy was undermined by ungentlemanly insiders or uncooperative outsiders. Even a tightly organized combination like the international oil cartel was continually plagued by periodic outbreaks of competition. The rubber cartel found that restrictive production quotas on the large plantations would be more than offset by the increased output of small, non-member producers. Similarly, under the NRA, enforcement of code prices and quotas was more easily conceived in theory than achieved in practice. Despite the rather severe penalties for violation of the codes of "fair competition," there was a considerable number of "unethical chiselers" who rendered them unworkable. Finally, even in an industry which is completely monopolized there is still room for rather sharp *intra*-firm competition between the operating divisions of the monopoly.

The question remains therefore: how much competition must there be to qualify an industry as "workably competitive," or how much monopoly must be shown before antitrust action is justified? The workable competition advocates do not provide an answer. Nowhere do they cite a specific example of an American industry which is too monopolistic to be considered workably competitive. This is an ominous sign for the employment outlook in the market for antitrust lawyers.

Workable Competition—a Cornucopia of Escape Hatches

Before the courts could decree a violation of Section 2 under the standard of workable competition, there would have to be proof that defendants possessed monopoly power, *and* that defendants' course of conduct was inconsistent with such tests of market performance as conservation of resources, employee welfare, promotion of foreign investment, maintenance of entrepreneurial incentives, and conditions favorable to national defense. As if the specifically enumerated tests of "good" performance (public interest) did not offer enough loopholes, the Business Advisory Council reminds us that these tests are "relevant, but not exclusive." We thus have the implicit assurance that should these performance standards fail to offer a sufficiently broad spectrum of defenses, others might be added to accommodate worthy defendants.

This almost preclusive reliance on market performance in judging the workability of competition raises at least two vexing problems. First, assuming that market performance in a particular industry is "good," the really significant question remains unanswered: have these favorable market results "been *compelled* by the system—by *competition*—or do they represent simply the dispensations of managements which, with a wide latitude of policy choices at their disposal, happened for the moment to be benevolent or 'smart'?"[16] In other words, are there checks, balances, and incentives *inherent* in workable competition which offer reasonable assurance that the workable competition of today will not become the abusive monopoly

[16] Lewis, "Symposium on the Antitrust Laws," 39 *Am. Econ. Rev.* 703, 707 (1949).

or oppressive conspiracy of tomorrow? Secondly, what evidence is there that "those predatory or collusive actions which the law [now] attacks are indeed requisite to a good performance." Is there not a *post hoc ergo propter hoc* aspect to the contention that where performance of an industry is "good," this is due to conduct in violation of the antitrust laws? As Professor Kahn points out, the burden of proof in this respect rests with the advocates of workable competition. To date, they have not shouldered the risk of non-persuasion with any degree of success.

Market Structure under Workable Competition

The workable competition standard, in its preoccupation with market performance, tends to ignore some crucial implications of market structure. In fact, workable competition assumes in part that, if monopolistic abuses and predatory practices can be controlled, an industry's market structure is of secondary importance. Thus the advocates of workable competition would generally agree with Justice McKenna's dictum that "the law does not make mere size an offense or the existence of unexerted power an offense."[17] They would disagree with Professor Stigler's generalization that "an industry which does not have a competitive structure will not have competitive behavior."[18]

This aspect of workable competition – the "abuse" theory of size – is open to several major criticisms. In industries showing a structural deviation from the competitive norm, an attack on monopolistic practices can be likened to a treatment of the symptoms while ignoring the disease. The history of the United Shoe Machinery Corporation is a case in point. After an unsuccessful dissolution suit, the courts perpetually enjoined the company's use of the tying contract. It was hoped at the time that this prohibition would remove the primary means of lessening competition and creating monopoly. This turned out to be a vain hope, however, for the company substituted other provisions in its leasing contracts to achieve the same unlawful ends. Finding the highway to restraint of trade blocked, the monopolist simply traveled cross-country. As a result, 25 years after the injunction decree, the Antitrust Division felt compelled to attack the industry's monopolistic structure, in order to deal effectively with its monopolistic practices.

Moreover, the "abuse" theory of size ignores the economic reali-

[17] United States v. U. S. Steel Corp., 251 U.S. 417, 451 (1920).

[18] "The Case Against Big Business," *Fortune,* May, 1952, pp. 123, 167.

ties of intercorporate relationships. Once a firm has attained a dominant position in the market place, it no longer has to engage in predatory practices to achieve its monopolistic ends. Its mere existence will be sufficient warning to smaller rivals that non-cooperation may be equivalent to suicide.[19]

Finally, it appears almost impossible to change oligopolistic market behavior without a transformation of oligopolistic market structure. This was dramatically indicated by defense counsel in the *Tobacco* case of 1946, who observed that the Court's decision left the companies "entirely without guide as to how they may lawfully avoid the creation of evidence of future Sherman Act violations against themselves, unless they cease business altogether." With justifiable consternation, counsel queried: "What are the specific policies and practices we must abandon, modify, or adopt in order to conduct our business according to law? . . . Is everything the appellants do illegal, or evidence of illegality, if done by more than one of them?" Neither the prosecution nor the courts provided an answer. The *Tobacco* case and similar prosecutions indicate the futility of condemning rational oligopoly behavior without an attempt to change the market structure which makes the condemned behavior almost inevitable.

The Vulnerable Basic Premise of Workable Competition

Workable competition rests on the unsubstantiated assumption that the present pattern of industrial concentration is an essential condition for efficiency and progress. According to the Business Advisory Council, "a big economy requires big industry. Without big enterprises, many constantly improved products cannot be turned out in

[19] Thomas Nixon Carver rejected the "abuse" theory in non-legal, but picturesque, language:

"If I may use a homely illustration, I will take the common house cat, whose diminutive size makes her a safe inmate of our household in spite of her playful disposition and her liking for animal food. If, without the slightest change of character or disposition, she were suddenly enlarged to the dimensions of a tiger, we should at least want her to be muzzled and to have her claws trimmed, whereas if she were to assume the dimensions of a mastodon, I doubt if any of us would want to live in the same house with her. And it would be useless to argue that her nature had not changed, that she was just as amiable as ever, and no more carnivorous than she always had been. Nor would it convince us to be told that her productivity had greatly increased and that she could now catch more mice in a minute than she formerly could in a week. We should be afraid lest, in a playful mood, she might set a paw upon us, to the detriment of our epidermis, or that in her large-scale mouse-catching she might not always discriminate between us and the mice." Carver, *Essays in Social Justice* 332 (1915).

the great quantities at the low prices that we Americans have come to expect—and demand." In a similar vein, Professor Oppenheim observes that "the real question is what form and degree of price competition can be *realistically expected under specified conditions of imperfect competition.*" As if the necessity of giant size had been scientifically established, the search is launched for a compatible degree of monopoly power rather than for a market structure which can yield more competition within the limits of modern technology.

To the writer's knowledge, no scientific study has yet demonstrated that giant size is imperative for the optimum utilization of modern technology or the attainment of efficiency in mass production industries. Indeed, some of the recent evidence has tended to point in the opposite direction. Fragmentary as it is, this evidence indicates, for example, that the giant U. S. Steel Corporation is no paragon of efficiency. A report prepared at the request of U. S. Steel itself pictured the corporation "as a big sprawling inert giant, whose production operations were improperly coordinated; suffering from a lack of a long-run planning agency; relying on an antiquated system of cost accounting; with an inadequate knowledge of the costs or of the relative profitability of the many thousands of items it sold; with production and cost standards generally below those considered everyday practice in other industries; with inadequate knowledge of its domestic markets and no clear appreciation of its opportunities in foreign markets; with less efficient production facilities than its rivals had; slow in introducing new processes and new products. On the basis of this powerful indictment, as well as other equally devastating evidence, some of our foremost economists concluded that the dissolution of U. S. Steel into at least three separate integrated units would not violate the demands of modern technology. They assured the Celler Committee: "One can be opposed to economic bigness and in favor of technological bigness in most basic industries without inconsistency. . . ."

The experience under Section 11(b) of the Public Utility Holding Company Act of 1935 is also noteworthy. It indicates that the comprehensive dissolution program under this Act did not preclude the optimum utilization of modern technology nor precipitate the fatal loss of efficiency which had been widely predicted prior to the law's passage. While the statistics are by no means conclusive, they do show that in most cases efficiency increased after dissolution, and that this increase was reflected in the security values of those operating companies which were divorced from their parent organizations. . . .

CONCLUSION

In conclusion, it may be well to remember that it is an *antitrust* law we are concerned with. The Sherman Act, as a charter of economic freedom, demands the promotion of more competition rather than the perpetual supervision of the policies and practices of monopoly. The Act is based on the theory that enforcement of competition "would contribute far more to the public interest in the level of costs and prices and in the economic allocation of capital than a programme of continuous surveillance of the business conduct of monopoly."[20] In this sense, the Act is more than an instrument of trade regulation; it is an expression of a uniquely American political philosophy.

No one can deny that there are unresolved problems in applying the per se doctrine of Section 1 and the market structure test of Section 2. It cannot be argued, however, that the twin approach of workable competition and the rule of reason is well calculated to resolve these problems in a manner consistent with traditional antitrust objectives. The proposed approach fails to provide an adequate guide for public policy and, more importantly, may lead to the eventual marasmus of basic antitrust safeguards. In the final analysis, the proposed approach stands for a proposition long ago diagnosed by Mr. Dooley: "The trusts are hideous monsters. On the one hand, I would stamp them under foot; on the other hand, not so fast."

[20] Rostow, "Britain and Monopolies," *Manchester Guardian*, Feb. 16, 1953, p. 4, [Editor's note].

PART TWO

POWER, INTENT, AND ILLEGALITY

INTRODUCTION

In analyzing some of the landmark decisions of 1946–48, Dean Rostow finds the crucial criterion in rule of reason cases to be the mere existence of economic power "substantially to influence" prices. Arguing that the Sherman Act forbids certain specific market situations, he considers the role of intent to exercise power to be limited. Where a proscribed degree of power to control prices or to exclude competition exists, the intent to achieve that power may be conclusively inferred from the mere existence of that power: "people intend the consequences of what they do." Where that power has been sought, but not yet achieved, intent becomes a more important ingredient in analyzing conduct. In other words, to prove a charge of "monopolize," power is enough; to prove "attempt to monopolize" requires power plus something else, namely, direct evidence of intent or behavior from which that intent may be inferred. In Rostow's view, conspiracy in oligopoly situations can be demonstrated without recourse to proof of direct or indirect communication among the alleged conspirators. Parallelism of action inferred from a course of dealings is sufficient evidence.

Professor Kahn, in contrast, finds that it is not the mere existence of power which is proscribed by the Act, but rather its exercise. Further, he considers that perhaps mere exertion of power is not enough; rather, power must be used "in such a way as to impose an unreasonable handicap on competitors." To show such unreasonable use of power requires proof of intent to do so. Thus, according to Kahn, illegality under Section 2 of the Act depends upon both the existence of power and the intent to use it.

It should be emphasized that while Rostow and Kahn disagree on the relevant criteria of illegality, they are both firm in their advocacy of a strong Sherman Act, and hence have much more in common with Adams than with Oppenheim.

EUGENE V. ROSTOW

Monopoly under the Sherman Act: Power or Purpose?*

> I will now tell you what I do not like [in the Constitution]. First, the omission of a bill of rights, providing clearly, and without the aid of sophism, for freedom of religion, freedom of the press, protection against standing armies, restriction of monopolies, the eternal and unremitting force of the habeas corpus laws, and trials by jury in all matters of fact triable by the laws of the land, and not by the laws of nations.
>
> THOMAS JEFFERSON *to James Madison, Paris, December 20, 1787*[1]

THE recent cases have radically altered the scope of the idea of monopoly—or, more precisely, of "monopolizing," since the statute uses the verb—the activity condemned by Section 2 of the Sherman Act.[2] The legal redefinition of monopoly opens new perspectives,

* From Eugene V. Rostow, "Monopoly under the Sherman Act: Power or Purpose?," *Illinois Law Review*. Reprinted by special permission of the *Illinois Law Review*, Copyright © 1949 by Northwestern University School of Law, Volume 43, Number 6, pp. 745–793. Reprinted also by permission of the author.

1 Thomas Jefferson, *Life and Selected Writings* (Modern Library Edition, 1944) 437.

2 United States v. Paramount Pictures, Inc., 334 U.S. 131 (1948); Schine Chain Theatres, Inc. v. United States, 334 U.S. 110 (1948); United States v. Griffith, 334 U.S. 100 (1948); Mandeville Island Farms v. American Crystal Sugar Co., 334 U.S. 219 (1948); FTC v. Cement Institute, 333 U.S. 683 (1948); United States v. Columbia Steel Co., 334 U.S. 495 (1948).

new doubts, and new possibilities of action under the Sherman Act. It is not too much to say that the current revision of Section 2 presents the central issue of doctrine in the entire field of anti-trust law — the concept of market control, which has increasingly become the chief, and often the only issue in anti-trust litigation. The problems arising under Section 2 are closely linked to those of Section 1, and the way in which Section 2 of the Sherman Act develops will inevitably affect the handling of many other categories of controversy under different sections of the statutes. For the propositions of policy which define the scope of Section 1 and Section 2 of the Sherman Act are the animating and decisive ideas of the whole body of law which has grown to such massive proportions during the last twenty-five years of anti-trust administration. That process of growth has helped to eliminate much that was extraneous to the broad purposes of the anti-trust laws, and to reformulate their chief propositions in ways which are not only more consistent and coherent than in the past, but as well more directly responsive to the underlying policy of the statute.

Strictly speaking, the potentialities of the Supreme Court's recent views are not really new. They go back in part to the theory of the Sherman Act expounded by Chief Justice White in his fundamental opinions on the rule of reason,[3] and they have many prototypes among the decisions of the period which ended with *United States v. United States Steel Corporation.* Like much of our present day law, the newer Sherman Act cases seem to reject the basic attitudes which prevailed during the 'twenties, and derive in considerable part from the philosophy of an older generation. The newer decisions are incompatible with the reasoning and spirit of the *United States Steel* case and a few of its companion pieces, but they rest quite securely on an earlier tradition of construing the statute. Psychiatrists tell us that much of the impulse for change in life comes from the need of children to become independent of their parents, and especially their fathers: a melancholy thought for parents, law teachers, and other elders of the community. Perhaps this drive is a clue to the endless cycle of opposites we see in the history of philosophy, politics, literature, and law, where classic follows romantic, mysticism succeeds realism, and the "New Look" sweeps away the old, but invariably restores the older. Whatever the subconscious source, the fact remains

[3] Standard Oil Co. of New Jersey v. United States, 221 U.S. 1 (1911); United States v. American Tobacco Co., 221 U.S. 106 (1911).

that in interpreting the Sherman Act, the Supreme Court seems to have discarded one set of its ancestors in favor of another.

* * *

II

The basic problem of defining monopoly power was considered in the first big controversy to emerge under the Act—the debate over the "rule of reason." The rule of reason was persistently advanced in dissent by Justice White for more than a decade, and finally became the prevailing view in 1911, after changes in the personnel of the Court gave him the opportunity to prevail. What is usually said about the controversy is misleadingly simple: White's victory eliminated the doctrine, supported by Taft, Peckham and Harlan, that the Act dealt with all the classes of arrangements which had been known to the common law, or which might be recognized in the common law process of adjudication, as restraints of trade or monopolies. For this concept of an all-inclusive Sherman Act, qualified only by its limitation to restraints which bore "directly" rather than "indirectly" on the national commerce, the Court substituted the rule that the courts should hold illegal under the Act only such restraints as were "unreasonable," in the Court's view of the circumstances.

The first opinions on the rule of reason, however, go far beyond the abstraction of their major premise. In the first place, White's view of the Act rested on the vitally important proposition that the Sherman Act did much more than enact the common law of restraint of trade for the federal area. The common law and its history, he said, constituted a background for the terms of the Act. But the language and scope of the Act were not limited by the history of the common law. The words were used in their practical and popular sense, and not as rigid legal terms of art; they were to be interpreted in the light of the overriding public policy of the Act, as "an all-embracing enumeration to make sure that no form of contract or combination by which an undue restraint of interstate or foreign commerce was brought about could save such restraint from condemnation."[4] Here White differed sharply and significantly with Holmes, who had argued with considerable force that the Act had nothing to do with competition, but that its purpose was to prevent the ruthless and exclusionary tactics of robber barons, whose behavior threatened the right of individuals to enter or to continue in callings of their

[4] 221 U.S. 1, 59–60 (1911). . . .

choice. In White's view, therefore, the rule of reason did not give the judges unfettered discretion to limit the Act to behavior they thought unreasonable. What was "reasonable," and hence legal under the rule of reason, was to be judged primarily in the light of the purpose of the Act. And the purpose of the Act, he emphasized, was to protect the public broadly against any "acts which, although they did not constitute a monopoly, were thought to produce some of its baneful effects."

Secondly, White's practical view of the problem of statutory interpretation presented by the Sherman Act led him to assimilate Sections 1 and 2 in a way whose implications are only lately becoming evident.

> [A] consideration of the text of the second section serves to establish that it was intended to supplement the first and to make sure that by no possible guise could the public policy embodied in the first section be frustrated or evaded. . . .
>
> Undoubtedly, the words "to monopolize" and "monopolize" as used in the section reach every act bringing about the prohibited results. The ambiguity, if any, is involved in determining what is intended by monopolize. But this ambiguity is readily dispelled in the light of the previous history of the law of restraint of trade to which we have referred and the indication which it gives of the practical evolution by which monopoly and the acts which produce the same result as monopoly, that is, an undue restraint of the course of trade, all came to be spoken of as, and to be indeed synonymous with, restraint of trade. In other words, having by the first section forbidden all means of monopolizing trade, that is, unduly restraining it by means of every contract, combination, etc., the second section seeks, if possible, to make the prohibitions of the act all the more complete and perfect by embracing all attempts to reach the end prohibited by the first section, that is, restraints of trade, by any attempt to monopolize, or monopolization thereof, even although the acts by which such results are attempted to be brought about or are brought about be not embraced within the general enumeration of the first section.

Against the background of these propositions, the Chief Justice plunged into the *Standard Oil* case.

The facts showed, he concluded, that the guiding spirits of the Standard Oil group had combined a large number of separate corporations and partnerships into the Standard Oil Company of Ohio, and later enlarged the scope of the combination through a trust agreement which unified the management policies of all the participating entities. This agreement was held illegal by the Supreme Court of Ohio in 1892, and in 1897 contempt proceedings in Ohio were begun on the ground that the defendants had failed in good faith to comply with the decision of 1892. The Standard Oil Company of New Jersey was thereafter reorganized as a holding company, and stock in the participating corporations of the Standard Oil combination was transferred to it. In addition to its allegations of growth to great size through combination and merger, the government had "set forth various means by which . . . in addition to the effect occasioned by the combination of alleged previously independent concerns, the monopoly and restraint complained of were continued." This latter class of averments deal with

> rebates, preferences and other discriminatory practices in favor of the combination by railroad companies; restraint and monopolization by control of pipe lines, and unfair practices against competing pipe lines; contracts with competitors in restraint of trade; unfair methods of competition, such as local price cutting at the points where necessary to suppress competition; espionage of the business of competitors, the operation of bogus independent companies, and payment of rebates on oil, with the like intent; the division of the United States into districts and the limiting of the operations of the various subsidiary corporations as to such districts so that competition in the sale of petroleum products between such corporations had been entirely eliminated and destroyed; and finally reference was made to what was alleged to be the "enormous and unreasonable profits" earned by the Standard Oil Trust and the Standard Oil Company as a result of the alleged monopoly; which presumably was averred as a means of reflexly inferring the scope and power acquired by the alleged combination.

These allegations, the Court concluded, had been substantially proved.

There is in the opinion a marked distinction between the fact that a gigantic corporation had been created to dominate the entire industry, and the various trade practices which the Court considered coercive, oppressive, or unduly restrictive. The judgment below was affirmed, the Court said, for two reasons:

> (*a*) Because the unification of power and control over petroleum and its products which was the inevitable result of the combining in the New Jersey corporation by the increase of its stock and the transfer to it of the stocks of so many other corporations, aggregating so vast a capital, gives rise, in and of itself, in the absence of countervailing circumstances, to say the least, to the *prima facie* presumption of intent and purpose to maintain the dominancy over the oil industry, not as a result of normal methods of industrial development, but by new means of combination which were resorted to in order that greater power might be added than would otherwise have arisen had normal methods been followed, the whole with the purpose of excluding others from the trade and thus centralizing in the combination a perpetual control of the movements of petroleum and its products in the channels of interstate commerce.
>
> (*b*) Because the *prima facie* presumption of intent to restrain trade,

to monopolize and to bring about monopolization resulting from the act of expanding the stock of the New Jersey corporation and vesting it with such vast control of the oil industry, is made conclusive by considering, 1, the conduct of the persons or corporations who were mainly instrumental in bringing about the extension of power in the New Jersey corporation before the consummation of that result and prior to the formation of the trust agreements of 1879 and 1882; 2, by considering the proof as to what was done under those agreements and the acts which immediately preceded the vesting of power in the New Jersey corporation as well as by weighing the modes in which the power vested in that corporation has been exerted and the results which have arisen from it.

These disapproved acts, which helped to confirm the *prima facie* case based mainly on size, were viewed, the Chief Justice said, "solely as an aid for discovering intent and purpose." This purpose he defines later as one "to exclude others . . . frequently manifested by acts and dealings wholly inconsistent with the theory that they were made with the single conception of advancing the development of business power by usual methods, but which, on the contrary, necessarily involved the intent to drive others from the field and to exclude them from their right to trade, and thus accomplish the mastery which was the end in view."

There is a duality in the reasoning of the *Standard Oil* and similar opinions, in the light of present day cases. On the one hand there is a recurring emphasis on intent and purpose to violate the act by gaining "economic mastery," evidenced by trade practices which the Court calls "new," "oppressive," "predatory," or "not normal" or "usual" means of growth. Nevertheless there is equally a recognition that "economic mastery" once achieved, and by whatever means achieved, "gives rise, in and of itself, in the absence of countervailing circumstances, to say the least, to the *prima facie* presumption of intent and purpose to maintain the dominancy over" the industry in question. Thus the early cases sharply distinguish the Sherman Act problem where a prohibited degree of market power has been achieved from those in which there is no more than an attempt to gain what is loosely called market domination. The application of the Act to the first class of cases is aided by what White had called "a prima facie presumption, to say the least," whereas in the second class far-reaching evidence of "intent" to achieve market control is required. While there were few cases which explored the nature of Chief Justice White's presumption in detail, his own reference to the earlier *Freight Association* and *Joint Traffic* decisions makes clear the implications of his view. In disaffirming the general theory of those cases, he strongly supported their holdings, in language which became the doctrinal basis of the line of decisions from the *Trenton Potteries* case to *United States v. Socony-Vacuum Co.*, and the entire conception that certain practices or arrangements could be held illegal per se under the Act without further enquiry into their reasonableness. The early railroad cases, it will be recalled, involved the association of independent railroads in a combination, through which their management policies were coordinated in many particulars, notably as to freight rates.

> [I]n the cases relied upon it having been found that the acts complained of were within the statute and operated to produce the injuries which the statute forbade, . . . resort to reason was not permissible in order to allow that to be done which the statute prohibited. This being true, the rulings in the cases relied upon when rightly appreciated were therefore this and nothing more: that as considering the contracts or agreements, their necessary effect and the character of the parties by whom they were made, they were clearly restraints of trade within the purview of the statute, they could not be taken out of that category by indulging in general reasoning as to the expediency or non-expediency of having made the contracts or the wisdom or want of wisdom of the statute which prohibited their being made. That is to say, the cases but decided that the nature and character of the contracts, creating as they did a conclusive presumption which brought them within the statute, such result was not to be disregarded by the substitution of a judicial appreciation of what the law ought to be for the plain judicial duty of enforcing the law as it was made.[5]

Thus the "prima facie presumption, to say the least," of the *Standard Oil* case becomes a "conclusive presumption" where a certain degree of control over price and other market policies is achieved, without reference to the "normality," "coerciveness" or the "predatory" character of the steps through which the forbidden quantum of market power is secured. Arrangements for fixing prices or dividing markets were in themselves unreasonable restraints of trade, for what they did, not what they were "intended" to do.

Certainly in the period before the *Steel* case, it was prevailingly held and understood that the acquisition of a certain degree of economic power was itself a violation of Section 2 and of Section 1, without particular evidence of how the power had been acquired or exercised. Considerations of "intent" became relevant when market power had not been achieved, and the problem for the court was to determine whether ambiguous conduct was part of a concerted plan

[5] 221 U.S. 1, 65 (1911). . . .

designed to achieve monopoly power in a market. Thus a man could speculate in grain futures without violating the Sherman Act, but not if his purchases and sales were steps in running a corner. It is true that in many but not all of these cases there was evidence of the kind of business behavior discussed in the *Standard Oil* case as helping to substantiate the prima facie case of illegality: — on the one hand, methods of growth, which seemed novel and abnormal when compared with expansion from within, and on the other, practices which offended the sensibilities of the Court, like espionage, secret rebates, and the like. But these were the formative years of the Sherman Act, and the government could not afford the risk of a test case resting on a particular theory. Thus Judge Learned Hand, in his opinion in *United States v. Corn Products Refining Co.*, decided in 1916, discusses the state of the law in terms which match the latest decisions of the Supreme Court. While the opinions of the Supreme Court, he said, left room for argument, the development of the cases seemed to support the view that the test of legality was "power only and not the manner of its exercise."

> If the decisions of the Supreme Court are to be so understood, it is the mere possession of an economic power, acquired by some form of combination, and capable, by its own variation in production, of changing and controlling price, which is illegal. . . . Under such an interpretation of the Act, Corn Products Refining Company is certainly a combination in restraint of trade, and its excuse is irrelevant, if it were true, that it has had a beneficent effect upon the industry. If the statute condemns an industrial integration of producing units sufficient to fix prices, so long as the total producing capacity remains unchanged, that policy must be respected and enforced, whether it is a good one or a bad.

On the other hand, Judge Hand points out, there are situations where the condemned degree of power may not exist, or where the exercise of power is considered relevant — for example, in applying the theory that it is the exercise and not the existence of the power which is decisive under the Act:

> . . . The intent of the combination so often appears in the cases as the determinating factor in illegality. It is not because unfair competition is a crime, but only because a monopolistic intent is the clearest evidence that the competition attempted is shown to be temporary and local, and that there is on this account a reasonable expectation that it will be succeeded by competition which the newcomer might well be able to meet, had his development been all the while left unimpeded. If that temporary or local competition were not coupled with such an intent, if there were honest grounds for supposing that it would or could remain to the per-

manent advantage of the consumer, the public would have no ground to complain, so long as the organization of industry remains on a competitive basis. The intent is the touchstone, not because we are concerned with moral delinquency, but with a test of the probable persistence of the combination's course of conduct.

Judge Hand's distinction between situations where a prohibited degree of economic power exists, and those in which it is sought, appears sharply in several of the major decisions of that era, notably the *Union Pacific* and *Southern Pacific* cases, where dissolution was decreed, and the *St. Louis Terminal* case, where the court ordered the unified terminal company for St. Louis to offer its facilities to non-participating roads, or be dissolved. There was no evidence in these cases of the kind of trade tactics discussed in *Standard Oil Co. v. United States,* or the first *Tobacco* case. They were sober and direct combinations, accomplished without melodrama. They were deemed illegal because in each case the scope of the combination created the power, in the Court's view, "to suppress or stifle competition or to create monopoly,"[6] in substantial if local segments of the economy. There was little or no mention of intent as a separate problem. The principle of these cases, the court said, is not simply that the combination might eliminate existing competition between the companies being brought together.

Such combinations, not the result of normal and natural growth and development, but springing from the formation of holding companies, or stock purchases, resulting in the unified control of different roads or systems, naturally competitive, constitute "a menace to, and a restraint upon, that freedom of commerce which Congress intended to recognize and protect, and which the public is entitled to have protected." *Northern Securities Co. v. United States,* 193 U. S. 197, 327 . . .

These cases, collectively, establish that one system of railroad transportation cannot acquire another, nor a substantial and vital part thereof, when the effect of such acquisition is to suppress or materially reduce the free and normal flow of competition in the channels of interstate trade.[7]

The two principal cases usually regarded as incompatible with this tradition of interpreting Section 1 and 2 are *United States v. United States Steel Co.,* and *United States v. International Harvester Co.* And certainly the philosophy of decision in the majority opinions of those cases is quite markedly different from that in some, and perhaps all of the earlier cases. The court said, and doubtless

[6] United States v. Union Pacific R. R. Co., 226 U.S. 61, 88 (1912).

[7] United States v. Southern Pacific Co., 259 U.S. 214, 230–231 (1922).

meant, that "the law does not make mere size an offense, or the existence of unexerted power an offense." The government's position is pilloried:

> The Government, therefore, is reduced to the assertion that the size of the Corporation, the power it may have, not the exertion of the power, is an abhorrence to the law, or as the Government says, "the combination embodied in the Corporation unduly restrains competition by its *necessary effect,* [the italics are the emphasis of the Government] and therefore is unlawful regardless of purpose." "A wrongful purpose," the Government adds, is "matter of aggravation." The illegality is statical, purpose or movement of any kind only its emphasis. To assent to that, to what extremes should we be led? Competition consists of business activities and ability — they make its life; but there may be fatalities in it. Are the activities to be encouraged when militant, and suppressed or regulated when triumphant because of the dominance attained? To such paternalism the Government's contention, which regards power rather than its use the determining consideration, seems to conduct. Certainly conducts we may say, for it is the inevitable logic of the Government's contention that competition must not only be free, but that it must not be pressed to the ascendency of a competitor, for in ascendency there is the menace of monopoly.
>
> . . . The regression is extreme, but short of it the Government cannot stop. The fallacy it conveys is manifest.[8]

Nonetheless, the decisions themselves, whatever their effect on public and legal opinion, do not support their doctrine. In cases of this order, technical distinctions are not of primary importance. But they have a place. And in the *Steel* case the determinative fact, the court said, was that the company had not in its opinion achieved monopoly power, having only 50% of capacity, and had given up the attempt to achieve monopoly power in view of the forces of resistance it met in the market. Although the Supreme Court agreed with two of the judges below that the United States Steel Company had been built by "illegal" tactics — i.e., by predatory and coercive acts designed to achieve a monopoly position, it felt that the Company's illegal purpose had been abandoned.

Similarly, in the *Harvester* case, the issue before the court was a limited one. The International Harvester Company had been formed in 1902 by combining 5 separate companies, comprising 85% of the national output of harvesting machinery, other competing companies being purchased thereafter. An anti-trust decree in 1914 ordered a

[8] 251 U.S. at 450–451.

dissolution of the company into three substantially equal and independent corporations. This decree was modified to provide that the business and assets be divided "in such manner and into such number of parts of separate and distinct ownership as may be necessary to restore competitive conditions and bring about a new situation in harmony with law." After several years of negotiation a consent decree was entered, in 1918, requiring the International Harvester Co. to limit itself to one agent in any city or town; to undertake to sell certain harvester plants; and to sell three of its harvesting machine lines to responsible manufacturers of agricultural implements who were unable to make harvesting machines. In 1923, the government moved to reopen the case, and to restore the original provision requiring a partition of the assets into three companies. Meanwhile, International's share of the harvesting machine market had dropped from 85% to 64% or less; independent companies had forged ahead, several testifying that the provision of the decree limiting International to one agent in each town had worked wonders; and the trial court found (one judge dissenting) that International lacked the power to dominate the market, to control prices or to exclude competition. The Supreme Court emphasized the fact that International had complied with and relied upon the consent decree of 1918, which gave the United States the right to further relief only in the event that competitive conditions had not been restored within 18 months after the end of the war. Here the case was brought more than 18 months after the end of the war. In any event, the Court concluded, International had lost both the power and the purpose to dominate the market. It was at this point in the development of its argument that the Court remarked that neither size nor unexerted power is an offense under the Act, and that price leadership does not alone "establish any suppression of competition or show any sinister domination."

The impact of the dicta in the *Steel* and *Harvester* cases was weakened by the language of *United States v. Swift & Co.,* where the meat packing companies sought to reopen a ten year old consent decree. That judgment, entered in 1920, kept the meat packers out of the business of dealing in dairy products or groceries, and of selling meat at retail, as well as the ownership or operation of stockyards or terminal railroad facilities. The sole issue for the Court, Justice Cardozo said, was "whether anything had happened that will justify us now in changing the decree." The court held that if the original decree was rational, so was its continuance, since no change of conditions was shown sufficient to impeach it.

> Mere size, according to the holding of this court, is not an offense against the Sherman Act unless magnified to the point at which it amounts to a monopoly (*United States v. United States Steel Corp.*, 251 U. S. 417; *United States v. International Harvester Co.*, 274 U. S. 693, 708), but size carries with it an opportunity for abuse that is not to be ignored when the opportunity is proved to have been utilized in the past. The original decree at all events was framed upon that theory. It was framed upon the theory that even after the combination among the packers had been broken up and the monopoly dissolved, the individual units would be so huge that the capacity to engage in other forms of business as adjuncts to the sale of meats should be taken from them altogether . . . We do not turn aside to inquire whether some of these restraints upon separate as distinguished from joint action could have been opposed with success if the defendants had offered opposition. Instead, they chose to consent, and the injunction, right or wrong, became the judgment of the court.

The court gives evidence at several points in its opinion that it did in fact support the theory of the original decree.

While these developments were occurring as to the significance of size under the Sherman Act, the Court was enlarging and expanding the doctrine of the *Trenton Potteries* case, that the power of a combination to fix price in a market was itself a violation of Section 1 of the Act, and perhaps of Section 2 as well. In *United States v. Socony-Vacuum, Inc.*, the court held that the illegal power need not be one to fix, or even to raise prices, but merely to influence them, or to prevent them from falling: "the placing of a floor under the spot markets obviously reduced the play of the forces of supply and demand . . . the thrust of the rule [of the *Trenton Potteries* case] is deeper and reaches more than monopoly power. Any combination which tampers with price structures is engaged in an unlawful activity. Even though the members of the price fixing groups were in no position to control the market, to the extent that they raised, lowered or stabilized prices they would be directly interfering with the free play of market forces. The Act places all such schemes beyond the pale and protects that vital part of our economy against any degree of interference." The factual situation in the *Socony-Vacuum* case illustrates how far the Court is willing to take the ban against arrangements effecting price – "the central nervous system of the economy." The combination involved in the case was temporary and informal. It carried out a policy which had been advocated by some government officers before the demise of N. R. A., and perhaps even afterwards. Yet no evidence as to the government's attitude was relevant, against the contention that combinations influencing price were illegal per se.

In its recent development, the doctrine of the *Socony-Vacuum* case threatens to engulf large segments of the earlier law under Section 1. The cement industry basing point decision, *Federal Trade Commission v. Cement Institute,* applies the theory of the *Socony-Vacuum* case on both its counts. It almost certainly marks the end of the *Maple Flooring* case and other landmarks in the law of loose combinations.

In the *Alcoa* case, Judge Learned Hand placed considerable reliance on this line of decisions. There the problem was whether the Aluminum Company of America, manufacturing (in Judge Hand's view) 90% of all the virgin aluminum produced in the United States, had violated Section 2 of the Act. If

> all contracts fixing prices are unconditionally prohibited, . . . the only possible difference between them and a monopoly is that while a monoply necessarily involves an equal, or even greater, power to fix prices, its mere existence might be thought not to constitute an exercise of that power. That distinction is nevertheless purely formal; it would be valid only so long as the monopoly remained wholly inert; it would disappear as soon as the monopoly began to operate; for, when it did — that is, as soon as it began to sell at all — it must sell at some price and the only price at which it could sell is a price which it itself fixed. Thereafter the power and its exercise must needs coalesce. Indeed it would be absurd to condemn such contracts unconditionally, and not to extend the condemnation to monopolies; for the contracts are only steps toward that entire control which monopoly confers: they are really partial monopolies.

The power over prices inherent in the size of Alcoa, in relation to the market as a whole, constituted a sufficient basis for the conclusion that it was violating the Act. Thus one part of the dictum of the *Steel* case necessarily falls: the decision in *Alcoa* means that *size* alone can be an offense under the Sherman Act, where size carries with it the degree of market power condemned by the Act. While presumably the Act, as a criminal statute, is inapplicable where such a degree of market power exists by inadvertence, an intent to keep the power will be freely inferred from its continued existence under normal commercial circumstances. A specific showing of intent to acquire monopoly power is required, Judge Hand said, only where monopoly power does not in fact exist; such cases, unlike the *Alcoa* case, are directed to nipping in the bud a course of conduct which has "the dangerous probability" of resulting in an injury to competition.

This analysis of the problem was approved by the Supreme Court in *American Tobacco Co. v. United States,* where the second part of the dicta of the *Steel* and *Harvester* cases was expressly repudiated. As a technical matter, the *Tobacco* case decided that a charge to the jury under Section 2 was not improper which described the offense in part as the possession by the three big tobacco companies of "the power to control and dominate interstate trade and commerce in a commodity to such an extent that they are able, as a group, to exclude actual or potential competitors from the field, accompanied with the intention and purpose to exercise such power." Evidence of the actual exclusion of competitors was not necessary. In short, it is the existence and not the exertion of power which the act condemns when the forbidden degree of power is coupled with an intent to use it. And the Court redefined monopoly power in the course of its opinion as the power "to raise prices or to exclude competition when it is desired to do so."

Without undertaking to repeat what I have said at length elsewhere about these two cases, I conclude that they stand for three broad propositions:

(1) Where a person or a group of persons acting together has the power substantially to influence the price of a commodity moving in interstate commerce, the existence of the power is illegal under Section 2, unless the defendant can show that the power has not been obtained or maintained deliberately – that is, for the purpose of enjoying and preserving the advantage of market position.

(2) The combination of several persons into a monopolistic group can be inferred from a course of dealings, and from their parallel action in response to the stimuli of the market, as well as from other evidence of their concert.

(3) An economic analysis of the position of defendants in their particular market settings is the key to measuring the degree of their control over price and output. In making such a determination, the courts will consider the extent to which market control may be the consequence of size alone, as in the *Aluminum* case; or the control of strategic factors in the market structure – like transportation facilities in the oil or the anthracite industries, or first run theatres in the movie industry; or the business position of the defendants in relation to existing or prospective competitors.

III

This view of the *Alcoa* and *Tobacco* decisions is confirmed, I should contend, by the three motion picture cases decided at the last term of the Supreme Court. Together they add a good deal of particularity to the law of the Sherman Act, in helping to identify the degree of market power the existence of which is deemed illegal; in clarifying the role of non-economic, or subjective ingredients in defining the offense under Section 2; and, above all, in asserting that where the offense is the acquisition of a forbidden degree of market power, not through loose association, but by reason of the size of business units, the normal anti-trust remedy is to reduce their size.

The most complex of these cases is *United States v. Paramount Pictures,* an equity proceeding against eight major companies, five of which produce, distribute and exhibit motion pictures, two being producers and distributors only, and one, United Artists, being exclusively a distributor. The complaint made distinct charges. The first was that the defendants as a group had attempted to monopolize and had monopolized motion picture production. On this issue, the trial court found for the defense, and the finding was not attacked on appeal. Secondly, the defendants were charged with conspiring to restrain and to monopolize the trade, and with restraining and monopolizing it, by together employing certain trade practices. These restrictive practices are considered under six sub-headings in the first part of the opinion, called "Restraint of Trade." There was a distinct charge of conspiring to restrain and monopolize, and of actually restraining and monopolizing, the exhibition of motion pictures in most of the larger cities of the country. The problem presented by this allegation is further considered by the Court in the third part of its opinion, headed "Monopoly, Expansion of Theatre Holdings, Divestiture." A further allegation was directed at vertical integrations as such, and another at the relations between the distributor defendants and exhibitors.

The main issue in the case, and in the motion picture business, the Court stated, is the exhibition of films in first-run theatres, particularly in larger cities. First-run showings are highly profitable—"the cream of the exhibition business," the Supreme Court said. The relative profitability of first-run exhibition, however, is the result of systematic policy, not technological imperative. A theatre after all is a first-run theatre only by the decision of the industry. A variety of trade practices give the larger theatres first-run privileges, and make such privileges valuable by preventing other theatres both from getting the same films for a specified time interval, and from showing them at less than a specified minimum price. By keeping the price in second-run theatres at or above a given point, it is possible to set the price in first-run theatres at a (higher) level, which takes full account of people's desire to see new films sooner rather than later.

These two interrelated trade practices—the establishment of minimum admission prices for runs subsequent to the first run, and the system of clearance, or time interval, arrangements — the District Court found to be unreasonable restraints of trade. Minimum admission price contracts were illegal on two grounds. First, the District Court inferred from the parallel behavior of the defendants that they had agreed upon a common policy towards admission price differentials between first and subsequent run theatres. This horizontal "conspiracy" to fix prices was held illegal on the analogy of *United States v. Masonite Corp.* and *United States v. United States Gypsum Co.*, as a plan to "regiment an entire industry," and thus unjustifiable even in the exploitation of valid copyrights. The distinction between the legitimate enjoyment of a patent monopoly, and the illegal regimentation of an entire industry through patent licenses, latterly much emphasized by the Supreme Court, does not bear analysis in many situations where the patent itself may be of commanding industrial importance. The weakness of the distinction, however, does not arise in the case of the movie industry, since the plan of distribution involved the combination of many independent copyrights, and the elimination or restriction of price competition between them.

Nor were the vertical price agreements between each major company and its licensee-exhibitors on a better footing. The precedent of the *General Electric* case[9] did not authorize separate vertical price fixing licenses which together constituted a system for eliminating price competition among exhibitors, and, more broadly, among copyrighted films.

Clearance arrangements which dealt with the timing of exhibition, though not admission prices, were considered on a different basis. The government had contended in the District Court that such provisions are illegal per se, like direct price-fixing clauses, since without them the first-run theatres would not be first-run theatres at all, and hence would not have the short period of monopoly which affords the movie industry the bulk of its revenue. The District Court did not agree, despite its conclusion that clearance arrangements did substantially affect admission prices. The holding below was (1) that the existing system of uniform clearances was illegal as a conspiracy in restraint of trade, the conspiratorial element being inferred either from participation in evolving the system, or acquiescence in it; but (2) that clearances reasonably restricted as to time and area, and limited to theatres in substantial competition with each other, would be permissible techniques for making money from the exhibition of a copyrighted film. The government did not challenge the District

[9] United States v. General Electric Co. 272 U.S. 476 (1926).

Court's conclusion, and the Supreme Court therefore refused to reopen the issue whether clearances were illegal per se, although it upheld the District Court's views against the defendants' challenge. In the light of the *Socony-Vacuum* case, and the Court's general suspicion of the movie industry, the point is at least doubtful.

There were other trade practices, the Court found, which unreasonably narrowed the area of competition among films, and among theatres. Joint management of otherwise competitive theatres, and joint ownership of theatres by one or another of the defendants, together with an independent interest, were considered at some length. Joint management was condemned outright. The discussion of joint ownership plans throws a good deal of light on the detailed meaning of the Court's theory of monopoly, for on this issue the District Court's ruling was reversed. So long as theatre ownership by the major companies is not totally forbidden, the Court said, (anticipating a later section of its opinion) the major companies should be required to sell to independents their interests in jointly owned theatres:

(1) Where the acquisition was the product of one or another of the industry's numerous violations of the Sherman Act;

(2) Where the interest was "innocently" acquired, but had been used to further the ends of the industry's general "conspiracy" against competition;

(3) Where the other party to the joint ownership would be an operator in the absence of joint ownership, since otherwise joint ownership would "afford opportunity to perpetuate the effects of the restraints of trade which the exhibitor-defendants have inflicted on the industry";

(4) Where, in the absence of any one of the conditions listed above, the joint ownership arrangement *results* in monopoly.

If the Court finds that neither monopoly nor unreasonable restraint of trade exist as a result of the ownership arrangements, the defendants might even be given permission to purchase the interest of their independent partners. The fourth proviso in this part of the opinion is a clear application of the Court's view that where monopoly, in the sense of economic power alone, exists in any appreciable part of the economy, it is illegal quite apart from its exercise, or any specific investigation of the purpose behind its acquisition or retention.

Block-booking was totally outlawed, as a device to use the demand for one copyrighted film as leverage to improve the market position of another. Such tying arrangements are as illegal between patents as in the cases where the right to use a patent is conditioned on the purchase from the patentee of an unpatented commodity or service.

* * *

The starting point of the case, the Court said, was a conspiracy to effect a monopoly through restraints of trade. It was therefore relevant in determining the need for divestiture, "to determine what the results of the conspiracy were even if they fell short of monopoly." However, the Court found, the key issue on the monopoly phase of the case was not the achievement of actual monopoly in all theatres (which the District Court had deemed to be its only problem under Section 2), but the degree of control by defendants in the first-run theatres. On this point there is no specific finding by the Court below, either for all first-run theatres, for first-run theatres in the 92 largest cities of the country, or for first-run theatres in separate localities.

The error of the Court below went deeper. The Court had found that the defendants lacked the purpose of achieving a national monopoly.

Second, we pointed out in United States v. Griffith, 334 U. S. 100, 68 S. Ct. 941, that "specific intent" is not necessary to establish a "purpose or intent" to create a monopoly but that the requisite "purpose or intent" to create a monopoly is present if monopoly results as a necessary consequence of what was done. The findings of the District Court on this phase of the cases are not clear, though we take them to mean by the absence of "purpose" the absence of a specific intent. So construed they are inconclusive. In any event they are ambiguous and must be recast on remand of the cases. Third, monopoly power, whether lawfully or unlawfully acquired, may violate §2 of the Sherman Act though it remains unexercised (United States v. Griffith, 334 U. S. 100), for as we stated in American Tobacco Co. v. United States, 328 U. S. 781, the existence of power "to exclude competition when it is desired to do so" is itself a violation of §2, provided it is coupled with the purpose or intent to exercise that power. The District Court, being primarily concerned with the number and extent of the theatre holdings of defendants, did not address itself to this phase of the monopoly problem. Here also, parity of treatment as between independents and the five majors as theatre owners, who were tied into the same general conspiracy necessitates consideration of this question.

Exploration of these phases of the cases would not be necessary if, as the Department of Justice argues, vertical integration of producing, distributing and exhibiting motion pictures is illegal *per se*. But the majority of the Court does not take that view. In the opinion of the majority the legality of the vertical integration under the Sherman Act turns on (1) the purpose or intent with which it was conceived, or (2) the power it creates and the attendant purpose or intent. First, it runs afoul of the Sherman Act if it was a calculated scheme to gain control over an appreciable segment of the market and to restrain or suppress competition, rather than an expansion to meet legitimate business needs. . . . Second, a vertically integrated enterprise, like other aggregations of business units . . . will constitute monopoly, which though unexercised, violates the Sherman Act provided a power to exclude competition is coupled with a purpose or intent to do so. As we pointed out in United States v. Griffith, . . . size is itself an earmark of monopoly power. For size carries with it an opportunity for abuse. And the fact that the power created by size was untilized in the past to crush or prevent competition is potent evidence that the requisite purpose or intent attends the presence of monopoly power. . . . Likewise bearing on the question whether monopoly power is created by the vertical integration, is the nature of the market to be served (United States v. Aluminum Co. of America, supra, 148 F. 2d at page 430), and the leverage on the market which the particular vertical integration creates or makes possible.

This crucial passage brings out the limits of the present status of the concept of intent or purpose under the Sherman Act. For the reasons indicated in the *Alcoa* case, among others, the Court is concerned to guard against the remote possibility of holding persons guilty of monopolizing under Section 2, especially in criminal cases, where their monopoly power exists by accident. For example, it would be extreme to prosecute under Section 2 the day after a valuable industrial patent expired, where the holder of the patent was the sole person to manufacture under it. And it seems similarly unlikely that a criminal statute would be invoked where all competition in a given line fell away through death, or bankruptcy, or fire. Curiously enough, there seems to be little corresponding feeling in equity cases under Section 1 that the offenses under Section 1, though equally criminal, must be accompanied by elements of intent. Price-fixing, tying clauses added to patents, arrangements for dividing the market, boycotts, resale price arrangements and the other common restraints under Section 1 are all considered without extended inquiry into intent. However, there is a distinct tradition to the effect that there must be some element of purposiveness about conduct violating Section 2 of the Sherman Act. But there are two distinct categories of intent: (1) the intent inferred from the existence of a forbidden share of economic power, however gained, on the familiar principle that people intend the consequences of what they do; and (2) a more deliberate and specific purpose to acquire a prohibited degree of economic power, relevant where such power is sought but not yet acquired. Intent in this sense is often inferred from systematic recourse to business tactics which themselves constitute illegal restraints of trade or are disapproved by the judges for unstated ethical reasons of their own. In the first case, where monopoly power is deemed to exist, the burden is basically on the defendants to rebut the presumption of a statutory purpose. Only in the second class of cases under Section 2 does it become pertinent to examine the defendants' conduct for evidence that they were engaged in a criminal attempt.

How "intent" became so vital a part of the literature of Section 2 of the Sherman Act is something of a mystery. It is clearly important where monopoly power is sought, but does not exist, for there the attempt is the offense. Where monopoly power in the sense of power over prices actually exists, by reason of the size of a single corporation, or the pooling for price purposes of the power of several dominant corporations, the policy of the *Socony-Vacuum* case doctrine seems to apply *a fortiori*. The existence of permanent arrangements creating such power over price come within the policy which condemned the temporary combinations in the *Trenton Potteries* case, and like situations, as illegal per se. Of course the proposition that at law intent is objective, not subjective, is at least as old as Mr. Justice Holmes. And the formula that the necessary degree of intent will be inferred from the existence of the power is orthodox. Complete verbal consistency is achieved by Chief Justice White, in his assertion that in cases of price fixing or the equivalent, intent is to be "conclusively presumed," i.e., is quite irrelevant. Thus with monopoly power defined as power over price, White's "conclusive presumption" of intent could finally assimilate the *Trenton Potteries* case doctrine with the problem of realized monopoly power under Section 2, and restrict the issue of intent to attempted monopolies, and to the remote situation of monopoly power "thrust upon" the monopolist.

Actually it is misleading and metaphorical to talk of either a "specific" or an "implied" intent to violate the Act, and the evidence commonly considered to show such intent has little to do with the problem. The Sherman Act largely concerns the behavior of business men, and their plans for making as much money as possible under the circumstances of their market position. Their desire to make money is hardly illegal – on the contrary, it is Adam Smith's "unseen hand," building economic efforts in the broadest social interest. The premise of our law and economics is that the response of business men to the possibility of profit assures society the best possible use of its resources, and the most rapid possible rate of economic progress. Where business men confront situations in which they can make money by organizing to eliminate competition, it is normal for them to do so unless restrained by law. There always appear to be larger and safer profits in monopoly — and more order, stability, dignity, power and peace, as well — than under the violent pressures of active competition. That the combination of business men into monopolistic patterns may be accomplished by "novel" or "abnormal" methods rather than by "normal" growth, has long since ceased to be important. The merger and the holding company are commonplace, as they were not when the *Standard Oil* case was decided. In *Appalachian Coals, Inc. v. United States,* Chief Justice Hughes pointed out that such distinctions were "artificial" and without substance. It should be equally irrelevant that the business program of combination might include steps otherwise illegal, like a boycott or a price fixing plan, or behavior regarded as brutal and tyrannous under the judges' private code of decorum in business. Business is not always a sport for gentlemen, and there is no reason for visiting the penalties of the Sherman Act on defendants merely because the judges would blackball them as candidates for a club. From the point of view of the purpose of the Sherman Act, the essential question is whether business men are taking advantage of their opportunities to combine, or of the structural character of their market, to gain monopoly profit. It is that result, or the quest for it, which is condemned by Section 2, just as Section 1 may outlaw some of the steps used on the way. The proof should be oriented, therefore, to the question whether a certain degree of economic power has been sought or achieved, not to the "normality" or "propriety" or "legality" of the means incidentally employed. A conspiracy, we are told, is a partnership in illegal purposes. The end sought — monopoly power — being illegal, any further evidence of illegality in the means used is redundant. The absence of oppressive, coercive or illegal behavior in the program of a business group cannot help to prove that the group lacks the intent to monopolize, whether "generally" or "specifically." As we have recently been reminded, the Act does not condemn "bad" trusts, and condone "good" ones.[10]

That this is a fair reading of the *Paramount* case seems to be confirmed by the *Schine* and particularly the *Griffith* decisions.

They were both equity cases brought by the United States against independently owned regional theatre chains, on the general charge that because of their bargaining power, and by reason of their close

[10] United States v. Aluminum Company of America, 148 F. (2d) 416, 427 (1945).

association with the major companies as a group, they were enjoying illegal advantages in their competition with smaller independents. In both cases the defendant chains had grown rapidly during the thirties, and included non-competing theatres scattered through many towns. In a majority of instances, the defendants owned or controlled either the only theatre, or all the theatres, in the community. In both cases, the defendants negotiated with the major companies for master agreements providing films for their chains as units, combining the buying power of their open and closed towns to obtain opportunities not available to their competitors, thus depriving competitors of films, putting them in unfavorable clearance categories, and the like. In the *Schine* case the defendants were charged with forcing sales of theatres by threatening to build competing theatres, "dictating terms" to distributors, exacting long term covenants not to compete from those who sold them theatres, and otherwise misbehaving. In the *Griffith* case, there was no such evidence, and the District Court found no purpose to use chain buying power for the purpose of eliminating competition and acquiring a monopoly of theatres in the competitive towns. Unlike the defendants in *United States v. Crescent Amusement Company,* the District Court found, the defendants had not even used the leverage of their position to insist on monopoly rights in towns where they had competition, by threatening to give a distributor no business in their closed towns.

The District Court was, however, reversed:

> It is, however, not always necessary to find a specific intent to restrain trade or to build a monopoly in order to find that the anti-trust laws have been violated. It is sufficient that a restraint of trade or monopoly results as the consequence of a defendant's conduct or business arrangements. . . . To require a greater showing would cripple the Act. As stated in United States v. Aluminum Co. of America, "no monopolist monopolizes unconscious of what he is doing." Specific intent in the sense in which the common law used the term is necessary only where the acts fall short of the results condemned by the Act. The classical statement is that of Mr. Justice Holmes speaking for the Court in Swift & Co. v. United States, 196 U. S. 375, 396:
>
> Where acts are not sufficient in themselves to produce a result which the law seeks to prevent — for instance, the monopoly — but require further acts in addition to the mere forces of nature to bring that result to pass, an intent to bring it to pass is necessary in order to produce a dangerous probability that it will happen. . . . But when that intent and the consequent dangerous probability exist, this statute, like many others, and like the common law in some cases, directs itself against that dangerous

probability as well as against the completed result. . . . And so, even if we accept the District Court's findings that appellees had no intent or purpose unreasonably to restrain trade or to monopolize, we are left with the question whether a necessary and direct result of the master agreements was the restraining or monopolizing of trade within the meaning of the Sherman Act.

Anyone who owns and operates the single theatre in a town, or who acquires the exclusive right to exhibit a film, has a monopoly in the popular sense. But he usually does not violate §2 of the Sherman Act unless he has acquired or maintained his strategic position, or sought to expand his monopoly, or expanded it by means of those restraints of trade which are cognizable under §1. For those things which are condemned by §2 are in large measure merely the end products of conduct which violates §1. Standard Oil Co. of New Jersey v. United States, 221 U. S. 1, 61. But that is not always true. Section 1 covers contracts, combinations, or conspiracies in restraint of trade. Section 2 is not restricted to conspiracies or combinations to monopolize but also makes it a crime for any person to monopolize or to attempt to monopolize any part of interstate or foreign trade or commerce. So it is that monopoly power, whether lawfully or unlawfully acquired, may itself constitute an evil and stand condemned under §2 even though it remains unexercised. . . . Hence the existence of power "to exclude competition when it is desired to do so" is itself a violation of §2, provided it is coupled with the purpose or intent to exercise that power. American Tobacco Co. v. United States, 328 U. S. 781, 809, 811, 814. It is indeed "unreasonable, per se, to foreclose competitors from any substantial market." International Salt Co. v. United States, 332 U. S. 392, 396. The antitrust laws are as much violated by the prevention of competition as by its destruction. United States v. Aluminum Co. of America, supra. It follows a fortiori that the use of monopoly power, however lawfully acquired, to foreclose competition to gain a competitive advantage, or to destroy a competitor, is unlawful.

A man with a monopoly of theatres in any one town commands the entrance for all films into that area. If he uses that strategic position to acquire exclusive privileges in a city where he has competitors, he is employing his monopoly power as a trade weapon against his competitors. It may be a feeble, ineffective weapon where he has only one closed or monopoly town. But as those towns increase in number throughout a region, his monopoly power in them may be used with crushing effect on competitors in other places. . . . Though he makes no threat to withhold the business of his closed or monopoly towns unless the distributors give him the exclusive film rights in the towns where he has competitors, the effect is likely to be the same where the two are joined. When the buying power of the entire circuit is used to negotiate films for his competitive as well as his closed towns, he is using monopoly power to expand his empire. And even if we assume that a specific intent to accomplish that result is absent, he is chargeable in legal contemplation with that purpose since the end result is the necessary and direct consequence of what he did. . . .[11]

Having found that monopoly power existed in both these cases, the Supreme Court sent the cases back with directions that the District Court draft new decrees based on the principle of divestiture. Far from being an extreme and punitive anti-trust remedy, the Court declared that in cases of monopoly a direct reduction in the size of the offending unit is the normal starting point in the decree:

In this type of case we start from the premise that an injunction against future violations is not adequate to protect the public interest. If all that was done was to forbid a repetition of the illegal conduct, those who had unlawfully built their empires could preserve them intact. They could retain the full dividends of their monopolistic practices and profit from the unlawful restraints of trade which they had inflicted on competitors. Such a course would make enforcement of the Act a futile thing unless perchance the United States moved in at the incipient stages of the unlawful project. For these reasons divestiture or dissolution is an essential feature of these decrees. . . .

To require divestiture of theatres unlawfully acquired is not to add to the penalties that Congress has provided in the anti-trust laws. Like restitution it merely deprives a defendant of the gains from his wrongful conduct. . . .

Decided by a safe majority of the Court, these three cases make clear both the character and the surprising scope of the new orthodoxy under Section 2.

In the first place, it is indisputable after these cases that the existence of what the Court will classify as monopoly power, coupled with a perfunctory and implied intent to use it, is illegal without reference to the techniques by which it was obtained. In the rare cases where the Court might condone the continued existence of such power, it is for the defense to prove that its blessings were thrust upon it.

As a matter of principle, it is difficult to come to another conclusion. The purpose of the Sherman Act is the broad public interest in protecting society and its members by preventing monopoly, and increasing the degree of competition in the structure of industry and commerce. The theory of the law is that competition promotes economic welfare and technological progress; provides the widest possible range of opportunities for individuals to become independent business men; and therefore constitutes the safest foundation for the class

[11] 334 U. S. at 104–108.

structure of society, maintaining a large and mobile middle class, within which economic power is widely dispersed rather than concentrated. If the economic result of monopoly power is achieved, why should the application of the Act depend upon the extrinsic circumstances that in gaining their power the monopolists may have violated a state statute, as in the *Northern Securities* case; or defied an order of a state court, as in the *Standard Oil* case; or extracted rebates, engaged in espionage or induced breaches of contract; or employed "novel" and "unusual" legal means of growth, such as holding companies, mergers, or trusts; or incidentally committed torts, like deliberately driving competitors out of business, through predatory price cutting or violations of other parts of the anti-trust laws, such as Section 1 of the Sherman Act, or the prohibition against price discrimination in the Clayton Act; or merely engaged in forms of business behavior the Court regards as "brutalities or tyrannies"? Such violations of law carry their own penalties. The second section of the Sherman Act should provide its distinct and independent measure of the offense it defines. The enforcement of Section 2 has often involved the serious remedy of directly reducing the size of large business units, and other far-reaching, even drastic steps. Such remedies should be imposed when the broad public purposes of the law require them. Their incidence can hardly depend upon a showing that the defendant company or companies have not only achieved what the court will regard as monopoly power, but have also engaged in a variety of practices – to an unspecified degree of importance – which can be classified as illegal, by virtue of laws other than Section 2 itself, or simply as ruthless or predatory by even vaguer and more subjective standards. The remedies under Section 2 should be employed when Section 2 has been violated, and not because the defendants may also have engaged in conduct made illegal by other laws, or regarded as improper for other reasons.

Perhaps more novel than the character of the doctrine in these cases is the range of its application. The Court has lately been emphasizing the availability of Sherman Act considerations in small segments and subdivisions of the economy. When the Court talks of "monopoly power," it seems to mean a rather limited degree of economic control in highly particularized markets. The definition of the commodity being monopolized in the *Alcoa* case was one of the most original parts of Judge Learned Hand's opinion. The market supply of which Alcoa produced 90% consisted of all the virgin aluminum produced and sold as ingots, plus the virgin aluminum fabricated by Alcoa, but not secondary and scrap aluminum used as an alternative source of ingots. The supply of secondary aluminum, the Court said, was within Alcoa's control over a period of years, if it consulted its self-interest. In the movie cases the markets being illegally dominated were sharply limited – the first run theatres of the large cities, or of any particular cities; the theatres of 76 towns in 6 states, in the *Schine* case, or of 85 towns in 3 states, in the *Griffith* case. *American Tobacco Co. v. United States* was concerned with monopoly in the national market for standard sized cigarettes, but not other forms of tobacco. In the *Columbia Steel* case the relevant markets were highly particularized, both geographically and in terms of the kinds of steel products being traded. *Mandeville Island Farms v. American Crystal Sugar Co.* dealt with the market for sugar beets in a small area of northern California. The *Yellow Cab* case concerned restraints in a small fraction of the national market for taxicabs, which itself is an insignificant part of the national market for automobiles. When coupled with the scope which the *Mandeville* decision gives to the Commerce Clause in Sherman Act situations, these cases bring the anti-trust laws into every corner of the economy, and make it as much a problem of small as of big business.

IV

If "the" market is to be defined for purposes of Sherman Act proceedings as the zone of immediate competition for the product of the defendant, what degree of economic control is necessary to constitute "monopolizing"? Under any theory of Section 2, monopolizing, after all, involves power as well as purpose, at least in cases which go beyond the stage of attempts. Indeed, where the requisite power exists, it is far more important than subjective evidence of purpose. What is the character of the economic power condemned by the Supreme Court as a violation of Section 2? . . .

In the *Alcoa* case, Judge Learned Hand was widely understood to correlate market power pretty much with capacity, despite the warning of the *United States Steel* case, and of the *Standard Oil* and *Pipe Line* decisions.[12] In measuring Alcoa's share of the market, he remarked that 90% "is enough to constitute a monopoly; it is doubtful whether sixty or sixty-four percent would be enough; and certainly thirty-three percent is not." Actually, his conclusion that Alcoa had 90% of the market capacity relevant to the legal issue of measuring market power rested on a non-arithmetic market analysis. Judge Hand's argument was that Alcoa should be considered to have

[12] The Pipe Line Cases, 234 U.S. 548, 559 (1914). . . .

90% of capacity because it controlled the market; it was not that it controlled the market because it had 90% of capacity. His evaluation of the market significance of secondary aluminum, and of ingots fabricated by Alcoa, and hence his finding of 90% capacity, can only derive from a prior conclusion that taking the market as a dynamic whole, Alcoa had every weapon of permanent economic power – size, the drive to seize new opportunities as they emerged, and a dominant relationship to existing or potential competitors.

The *Columbia* case supports this view of Judge Hand's analysis. The problem for the Court, the *Columbia* case asserts, does not end with a figure representing the defendant's fractional share of market capacity. The court must decide which part of the market is relevant to the charge – in the *Columbia* case the market in issue was defined both geographically and by product – and then examine its workings in detail to ascertain how decisions as to price and output are made. In this way the factors whose control gives leverage over the market are isolated, and a judgment becomes possible as to whether or not the defendants possess the degree of influence over price, and over the entry of competitors, which brings them within the policy of the Act. . . .

In the *Tobacco* case, the conclusion that a forbidden degree of monopoly power existed was based on the market influence of three major tobacco companies which together produced between 70% and 90% of the standard sized cigarettes. These companies followed the policy of price leadership which would be expected in a market so organized, both in their relations with the numerous sellers of tobacco and with the numerous wholesalers and retailers of cigarettes. It is true that in the *Tobacco* case the jury inferred from the conduct of the defendants that there was a conspiracy to monopolize a part of the tobacco industry – a conspiracy "to fix and control prices and other material conditions relating to the purchase of raw material in the form of tobacco leaf for use in the manufacture of cigarettes. It also appears to have been one to fix and control prices and other material conditions relating to the distribution and sale of the product of such tobacco in the form of cigarettes." The evidence, however, on which this inference of combination was based, was almost exclusively that each of the Big Three companies, entirely aware of their common stake in concerted action, moved in parallel lines. It was the kind of market behavior to be predicted analytically in any market organized in this pattern. And it is the kind of market behavior commonly found in such situations.

Doubt has been expressed whether the emphasis on this phase

of the element of conspiracy in the *Tobacco* case would not lead to an injunction against further conspiracy, rather than a decree of dissolution addressed to size and market power as such. If the prohibited degree of monopoly power exists only by reason of the combination of defendants, the argument goes, it can be dispelled by forbidding them to act "collectively," in the phrase of the *Paramount* case. Such doubts should have been reduced by the three movie cases of the last term, and particularly by the *Paramount* case. The *Paramount* case decides that as many as eight companies can together constitute a monopoly under Section 2, their combination being shown by their similar behavior, and their "acquiescence" in many practices. And the *Paramount* case strongly implies, if it doesn't flatly say, that a divestiture of theatre ownership by the major companies is the crucial provision of an adequate decree. . . .

One might contend that in the *Paramount* case the defendants were linked into a monopolistic group through what the Court repeatedly calls a conspiracy to restrain and monopolize, involving persistent recourse to illegal means of doing business. Actually, at many specific points, the conclusion of combination was reached as an inference from behavior. "It is not necessary to find an express agreement in order to find a conspiracy. It is enough that a concert of action is contemplated, and that the defendants conformed to the arrangement.[13] The remaining question, however, under circumstances where such traditional elements of illegality are lacking, is how closely defendants have to be connected in order to constitute a collective monopoly? Will the courts conclude that sellers are "conspiring," or at least combining, when they "are (almost) unaware of the facts"?

The legal problem of proof should be framed by the economic realities of the market situation. In many markets a large share of supply is produced and marketed by one firm or a small group of firms conspicuously larger than their competitors. In such markets customs or practices often exist which eliminate or severely restrict price competition. However such practices originated, their survival does not ordinarily depend on agreement, but on the common interest of the dominant sellers in avoiding price competition. Each seller has an equal interest in a policy of "live and let live," an equal distaste for "cutthroat competition." The dominant firm may announce its price, and others usually respond. . . . The effect of . . . is to substitute an administered price for a market price, with far-reaching conse-

[13] 334 U.S. at 142.

quences to output, and perhaps also to the rate of technological progress. Arrangements of this kind exist in great variety. Detail apart, however, they all represent an assumption by sellers (or buyers, in the case of markets dominated by a few large buyers) of the authority to make decisions about the level of prices and hence of output; these are peculiarly and notably the functions which the law expects to be performed by markets or by the government and not by individuals.

Where an industry is organized in this general way, price, output, and opportunities to enter the business are akin to those which would obtain under conditions of monopoly. The economic results, the social results, and the political results of the market structure are those which are condemned in principle by the Sherman Act. That is to say, the necessary consequence of the economic organization of the industry is that the large and dominant sellers, if they have a decent regard for their own interests, will act as if they had "combined," in the sense of the *Tobacco* and *Paramount* cases, although their officers may never have talked to each other, even on the phone or the golf course. The market power of the dominant firms is used "collectively," in the phrase of the *Paramount* case. Under such circumstances, why shouldn't the courts infer the required degree of combination from the fact that the economic power of the separate companies has been effectively combined for purposes of price policy, very much as the courts infer "statutory intent" to maintain a monopoly from the fact that monopoly power exists? And isn't such a process of inference close to being accepted practice today?

The effective economic pooling of market power should support the legal conclusion that the result was intended. In the *Cement* case, for example, evidence of monopolistic price uniformity was a powerful factor in supporting the Federal Trade Commission's inference of an agreement to maintain a basing point system, individual acquiescence in the plan being enough to show individual participation. True, in that case there was a trade association, and some evidence of action to police the plan. But the Supreme Court gave emphatic consideration to the nature of the price quoting plan, as a device for restricting price competition, and to the fact of price uniformity; and it quoted with approval a remark of the Seventh Circuit, to the effect that in the light of price uniformity itself, any conclusion other than that of a price fixing agreement "would do violence to common sense and the realities of the situation."[14]

[14] United States Maltsters Associations v. FTC, 152 F. 2nd 161, 164 (C.C.A. 7th, 1945).

Where the legal problem is to prove that economic power has been pooled, the best evidence should be an economic demonstration that such a pooling has occurred, for price purposes, rather than testimony as to coercive or illegal trade tactics supposed to prove "conspiracy."

The principal evidence relied upon in the *Tobacco, Paramount* and other recent cases to support an inference of combination would be equally available in many situations of central economic importance, where a few companies acting in parallel ways have a substantial degree of control over price in the market by reason of their size, and the fact that for purposes of price policy – "the central nervous system of the economy" – their economic power has been effectively pooled, with or without actual agreement. On the analogy of the *Paramount* case, their offense, viewed collectively, would be the possession and inevitable pooling of a forbidden degree of market power; and the basic remedy proposed by that case would be a direct reduction of the illegal market power by procedures of reorganization under judicial control.

The movie cases, then, seem to confirm and carry forward the doctrine of *Alcoa* and *Tobacco* decisions, to this effect:

1. The existence of a prohibited degree of economic power is illegal, whatever the circumstances of its origin or development, if it is accompanied by an intent to use it. This intent may be "conclusively presumed," if the analogy of the *Trenton Potteries* doctrine is accepted, or freely inferred from the existence of the power, as in the *Alcoa, Griffith* and other decisions;
2. In markets dominated by a few large sellers, their economic power will be viewed collectively, and the legal conclusion of combination will be inferred largely from the economic fact that a pooling of such power for price purposes has in fact taken place;
3. The normal remedy in cases of realized monopoly power is to reduce the size of the business units, so as to restore conditions of workable competition in the market.

* * *

CONCLUSION

Some of the justices of the Court, and other students of the development of the anti-trust laws, have expressed concern lest the Court, in dealing with the legality of modern forms of big business organization, undertake legislative decisions more properly within the discretion of the Congress. A historical view of the purpose and growth of the anti-trust laws should help to allay such doubts.

The Sherman Act has broad and simple goals. Congress contemplated that the Act prevent the social evil of monopolistic concentration of economic power, and affirmatively assure society the advantages of widely dispersed economic authority and opportunity. The procedure adopted, as Justice Reed has recently pointed out, was to delegate to the courts wide responsibility for applying the Act to changing economic conditions.[15] The far-reaching extent of judicial power under the anti-trust laws is part of the historical pattern of our constitutional practice, in which the judiciary has always exercised extraordinary authority. The statute itself "as a charter of freedom . . . has a generality and adaptability comparable to that found to be desirable in constitutional provisions."[16] It was designed to deal not only with the forms of monopoly which existed at the time it was passed, but with all the circumstances in which the problem of monopoly and restraint of trade might subsequently arise. In Chief Justice White's phrase, the Act was drawn to reach arrangements, whatever their form, which might be thought to produce "some of the baneful effects" of monopoly. Around the turn of the century, the dominant types of monopoly organization were trusts, mergers or other combinations which in many industries embraced all or almost all existing capacity. In oil, tobacco, whiskey, sugar, steel and other vital areas, a single combine made 90% or more of market supply. Moreover, in many cases, the dominant combination had reached its market position along a trail of rough and tumble tactics which have now become relatively rare. Since the middle twenties, increasingly, a totally new pattern of industrial organization has emerged in many industries. 60% to 80% of supply is produced by 2 or 3, or sometimes as many as 10 or 15 firms. Overt agreements among them are of diminishing importance, when compared with the heyday of trade association activities during the late 'twenties and early 'thirties. Ruthless and oppressive trade tactics are less common than in the past. The problem of prevailing importance in the most important sector of the economy is to formulate a policy towards the economic organization of markets, where, for purposes of price and output, the economic power of a few dominant firms is in fact pooled, in large part by the separate and parallel response of the big firms to their own interests, with results which approximate those which would obtain under monopoly.

In the last few years the Supreme Court has worked out a doctrinal basis for effective action to secure the great ends of the Sherman

[15] United States v. Columbia Steel Co., 334 U.S. 495, 526 (1948).

[16] Appalachian Coals, Inc. v. United States, 288 U.S. 344, 359–360 (1933).

Act in cases of this kind. It has directed attention to the necessity for a full analysis of actual market situations, in all their variety and complexity, to determine whether in fact private groups have acquired or maintained monopoly power over price. That power, the Court has said repeatedly, can be exercised either by a competitive market or by the government, never by private groups. Where such power is held by a single firm, its existence is illegal. Where it is achieved by direct combination, it is illegal per se, and intent to violate the statute is conclusively presumed. Where such market power is informally shared by a small group whose influence is in fact used in common to avoid price competition, their combination for purposes of the Sherman Act has been inferred largely from their market behavior. In these cases the pooling of the market power of the large sellers or buyers, with the result of monopolistic pricing, depends not on their actual agreement, but on the parallelism of their response to market forces, in view of their size and market position. It follows that the appropriate remedy, as in cases of monopoly achieved by a single firm, is not merely to forbid their association, but to reduce their size. The goal of such proceedings is to reorganize the industry into efficient smaller units, sufficiently numerous and independent so that the results of workable competition can reasonably be expected from the operation of market forces.

The purposes of the Sherman Act have not been fully realized in our economic life. Its history is one of futility and half-measures, of gallant attempts, occasional victories, frequent retreats, of false starts and missed opportunities. Above all, it is a history marked by the absence of any planned and systematic effort to gain the basic strategic ends of the statute. Cases are brought piecemeal, in response to the pressure of complaints, or the political winds. During the last few months, for example, we have witnessed a well-publicized antitrust attack on inflationary price rises, especially in the most competitively organized sectors of the economy. It would be hard to imagine a more complete misunderstanding of the problem of inflation, or a more complete waste of the time and energy of the Department of Justice and the Courts.

Not even the most optimistic and single-minded trust buster could expect the Sherman Act to become a revolutionary instrument. The existing structure of industry and commerce has enormous historical momentum. It contains many elements of monopoly, some protected by law. At the same time, there is still a good deal of scope for innovation and enterprise. New men and new ideas keep bursting through the neat fences of existing interests, either with new firms or new techniques. The problem is not one of choice between perfect competition and perfect monopoly. The issue for government and society is whether to invest considerable effort against vigorous resistance in order to alter the balance in favor of the competitive drives of economic and social life. The implications of the recent cases in the Supreme Court, if applied to some of the most important of our industries, could materially reduce the degree of concentration of economic power in society, and tend cumulatively to influence the development of industry in more competitive forms. One can readily see the vitality of anti-trust policy in various parts of the economy. The process of railroad consolidation was stopped before Hill or Harriman took over the entire railroad network of the United States. In the steel industry, Big Steel won its anti-trust case, but embarked on a policy of caution in growth, out of respect for the weapon which just missed being applied to it. And perhaps most striking of all, Alcoa's share of the aluminum market has dropped from 90% to 50% in a few years, as a result of a government policy for the disposal of war plants which was rooted in the tradition of the anti-trust cases. Much more can be done to increase the competitive character of the economy, by applying the newer conception of the Sherman Act to the principal industries and markets of the economy.

To guide the evolution of industry and commerce in a more competitive direction is one of the vital jobs of American democracy. It cannot be done without the support of the courts. But it cannot be done by the courts alone. Our chances of materially increasing the degree of competition in the economy at large depend on the ability of the Department of Justice and the Federal Trade Commission to conceive and carry out a program comparable in imagination to those of our strategic bombing operations during the war. Commodities, concentrations of power and market practices should be selected for litigation in order of their priority, on the basis of a dynamic analysis of the way in which the economy actually works. We can expect worthwhile results from our investment in the anti-trust laws only if they are directed against targets of general importance to the economy as a whole.

Our society depends on unregulated markets as its main institutions for allocating resources and income. If we wish to remain a democratic community, we have a large stake in keeping this function one for the market, rather than for government agencies, undertaking to direct the detail of business transactions throughout the economy. The transfer to government of general responsibility for allocating resources and fixing prices would seriously disturb the balance of social power among business, labor and the state, and materially reduce our expectations of continuing as a free society. The market, however, can do an effective and satisfactory job only if it is reasonably competitive. Our best hope of remaining a free society is to reorient our economic growth in a clearly competitive direction through the vigorous application of the anti-trust laws to our main current problem of monopoly — the structure of our major industries, led in many cases by a few dominantly large units. . . .

ALFRED E. KAHN

A Legal and Economic Appraisal of the "New" Sherman and Clayton Acts*

ACADEMIC economists have traditionally supported the basic purposes and underlying assumptions of the antitrust laws, stressing the feasibility and desirability of competition as the prime regulator of economic activity. Their major criticisms in the past have been directed not so much against the laws themselves as against the Supreme Court's adoption and application of a qualifying "rule of reason" in interpreting them between 1911 and 1936. Under this test, the illegality of big businesses did not depend on the enjoyment of monopoly power, but on whether or not defendants had obtained

* From Alfred E. Kahn, "A Legal and Economic Appraisal of the 'New' Sherman and Clayton Acts." Reprinted by permission of the copyright holder from *The Yale Law Journal,* Volume 63, Number 3, pp. 293–322, 327, 331–347. Single issues, as well as back issues available at $2.50 from Fred B. Rothman, 57 Leuning Street, South Hackensack, New Jersey. Subscription, $10.00 per volume available from Business Office, *The Yale Law Journal,* 401-A Yale Station, New Haven, Conn., 06520.

or exerted economic power "unreasonably" – *e.g.*, employing predatory competitive tactics – thereby evincing an "intent to monopolize." Many economists felt that the rule of reason rendered the law impotent.

The last decade has witnessed a striking reversal in judicial interpretation of the antitrust laws. There has been some tendency for the courts to dilute the rule of reason, creating a more effective "new" Sherman, as well as Clayton, Act.[1] This dilution has been manifested by a tendency to condemn per se business size, integration, and monopoly power. The courts have also been condemning such business practices and procedures as differential pricing, exclusive dealing, and tie-in agreements, on the ground that by these tactics the offending concerns, usually big and powerful sellers, have excluded or disadvantaged smaller competitors.[2]

Concomitant with these recent legal developments, academic economists have unleashed a "new criticism" of the antitrust laws. These "new critics" do not deny that the recent legal developments have made it easier for the antitrust authorities to win cases. But they question, with increasing boldness, whether the developments have not contravened rather than promoted the basic purpose of the laws.[3] They point out that big business is not just an inevitable evil but a necessary agent of effective competition in modern industrial society. A firm may emerge with a large share of the market because of its superior efficiency and enterprise. In the same way, exclusive dealing and full requirements contracts may be indispensable instruments or methods of competing under modern conditions. They contend, therefore, that the Supreme Court was on firm economic ground in the 1920's when it held, under the rule of reason, that business size and market power were not in themselves offensive; that the Clayton Act was justified in condemning the enumerated practices only if their "effect may be to substantially lessen competition"; and that the recent dilutions of these escape clauses have paradoxically permitted the

1 For an early and approving recognition of some of these tendencies, see Rostow, "The New Sherman Act: A Positive Instrument of Progress," 14 *U. of Chi. L. Rev.* 567 (1947); Rostow, "Monopoly Under the Sherman Act: Power or Purpose?," 43 *Ill. L. Rev.* 745 (1949).

2 For a detailed study of recent leading price discrimination cases, see Dirlam & Kahn, "Price Discrimination in Law and Economics," 11 *Am. J. of Econ. & Soc.* 281 (1952).

3 See, *e.g.*, Adelman, "Effective Competition and the Antitrust Laws," 61 *Harv. L. Rev.* 1289 (1948); Adelman, "Integration and Antitrust Policy," 63 *Harv. L. Rev.* 27 (1949).

authorities to harass enterprising big businesses in order to protect small and inefficient competitors, thus discouraging competition itself. These critics propose that the rule of reason be restored to its former vigor, and that antitrust decisions depend henceforth on the impact of the disputed market structures or practices on *workable* (as distinguished from pure or perfect) competition,[4] measured in terms either of concrete economic results or of the continuing vitality of competitive forces in the market as a whole.[5]

In appraising these criticisms, this article examines the recent antitrust decisions in a legal and economic context. The significant legal question is to what extent the traditional rule of reason has in fact been abandoned. The crucial economic question is whether the decisions have, as has been so often alleged, made for less effective competition. The article focuses on the recent antitrust cases involving business size and integration, and includes within its compass integration not only by financial control, but also by means of tie-ins, exclusive dealing, and full requirements contracts. All of these practices represent methods of obtaining or exercising some of the advantages conferred by integration, and have similar effects on competition. Underlying the entire discussion is the conviction that the legal criteria of unreasonable restraint and monopoly are always dictated primarily by the mores of a free enterprise society, rather than by the clear-cut requirements of optimum economic performance.

Business Size and Integration in Monopoly Cases

The Sherman Act was not intended to attack the mere enjoyment of monopoly power. Rather, the stigma of "monopolizing" has attached, traditionally, to the unreasonable *acts* incident to attempts to acquire or maintain substantial monopoly power. Indeed, the *American Can, United Shoe Machinery, U.S. Steel,* and *International Harvester*

[4] . . . The concept of workable or effective competition is necessarily imprecise and controversial. . . . Economists differ in the extent to which they would look primarily to an industry's *structure*, or to the *behavior* of the firms in it, or to its actual economic *results* to see whether it deserves approval as workably competitive, *i.e.*, as containing the best attainable balance of monopolistic and competitive elements.

[5] See . . . Oppenheim, "Federal Antitrust Legislation: Guideposts to a Revised National Antitrust Policy," 50 *Mich. L. Rev.* 1139 (1952). [Reprinted here; see pp. 2–35.]

In Kahn, "Standards for Antitrust Policy," 67 *Harv. L. Rev.* 28 (1953), the author described and appraised the possible alternative economic criteria of monopoly and monopolizing.

decisions all seemed to argue that even dominant firms — the result of mergers whose purpose was virtually to eradicate competition in their respective industries — could not be condemned or dissolved, if they had not achieved almost complete monopoly, and had not employed flagrantly oppressive methods. Recently, the courts have gone far to reverse this earlier attitude, and have applied Section 2 of the Sherman Act to monopolists whose actions were not found to be unreasonable or motivated by a clear intent to monopolize; oligopolists (a few dominant sellers), without clear evidence of collusion between them; integrated companies that excluded competitors merely from the patronage of their own integrated subsidiaries or of customers with whom the integrated companies had signed full requirements contracts; "hard bargainers" that enjoyed little monopoly power but undoubtedly enjoyed some strategic advantages over their smaller, non-integrated rivals.

"MONOPOLIZING" AS THE ENJOYMENT OF A MONOPOLY

The Alcoa and United Shoe Machinery Decisions

The beginnings of the "new" Sherman Act are customarily traced to Judge Hand's decision in the *Alcoa* case. After resolving the complex issue of how best to measure the company's share in the national aluminum market by selecting the combination of figures that yielded the highest possible percentage, Hand stated that Alcoa's ninety percent control "is enough to constitute a monopoly," and that "having proved that 'Alcoa' had a monopoly . . . the plaintiff had gone far enough." . . .

The basis on which Judge Hand chose to condemn Alcoa represented a substantial departure from the traditional rule of reason and its conception of monopolizing. One might argue that *Alcoa* was not particularly novel, since previous decisions exonerating big business defendants were heavily influenced by the fact that the defendants were not pure monopolists. But in previous decisions, the defendants had originally been put together by mammoth mergers that left them with preponderant shares of total national production. Had they retained those market positions, the courts would not have been justified in condemning them for monopolizing, "not as a result of normal methods of industrial development, but by new means . . . resorted to in order that greater power might be added than would otherwise have risen had normal methods been followed. . . ."[6] Judge Hand's

[6] Standard Oil Co. v. United States, 221 U.S. 1, 75 (1911). This was Chief Justice White's historic enunciation of the rule of reason.

decision, on the other hand, seemed to define monopolizing as the mere enjoyment of monopoly, even if attained entirely as a result of efficiency, foresight and technological innovations.

But *Alcoa* is not as revolutionary as it seems. Its condemnation of monopolies as such is explicitly confined to classic, single-firm monopolies. Professor Mason criticizes Hand's measures of Alcoa's market position – both the particular divisor and dividend that yielded the ninety percent quotient, and the identification of market control with percentage shares in a given product – as "very dubious economics."[7] The criticism is partially justified, since the ninety percent figure ignored the competition between Alcoa's virgin ingot and secondary aluminum, as well as other metals. But significantly, Mason offers no better economic measure. None is available. The figure of ninety percent was as indicative as any other of the unquestionable fact that one company had a very substantial range of discretion in the pricing and the rate of development of an entire industry.[8]

Another and more important reason for questioning the revolutionary character of the *Alcoa* and later *United Shoe Machinery* decisions is that the defendants had monopolized their respective markets in the traditional sense as well. Although emphasizing United Shoe Machinery's eighty-five percent market share, Judge Wyzanski plainly predicated his condemnation of the company on his finding that it had not attained and maintained its overwhelming strength solely by virtue of its "ability, economics of scale, research, natural advantages, and adaptation to inevitable economic laws." Rather, United Shoe Machinery's business policies, *i.e.*, its *actions*, while not inherently predatory or immoral, had erected arbitrary barriers to competition.

Judge Hand could have reached the same conclusion in *Alcoa*. It should not have been necessary to find a precise measure of Alcoa's market power in order to convict it under the antitrust laws. The economic assumption of those laws is that vigorous, fair competition in finding and satisfying customers will not result in a monopoly. The history of the aluminum industry, of the ways in which Alcoa obtained, retained, and used its market power, does not disprove this assumption. Alcoa might have enjoyed its predominant position in

[7] Mason, "The Current Status of the Monopoly Problem in the United States," 62 *Harvard L. Rev.* 1265, 1273–4 (1949).

[8] Muller, *Light Metals Monopoly* 21, c, 1, *passim* (1946). . . . Wallace, "Aluminum" in *International Control in the Non-Ferrous Metals* 210, 258 n.87 (Elliott ed. 1937) (hereinafter cited as Elliott).

the American market in 1944 without having bought out the Cowles Brothers and the critical Bradley patent in 1903, without the expressly exclusive clauses in its bauxite and power purchase contracts, annulled by a 1912 consent decree, without the acquisition of at least one imminently threatening domestic competitor in the 1920's, the squeeze on fabricators, and the direct and indirect understandings with foreign producers, including the strangely cooperative "competitor" Southern Aluminum Company. Its head start and advantages of "experience, trade connections, and elite of personnel" might alone have sufficed to discourage or destroy competitors. Neither an economist nor a lawyer can be sure. But in fact these actions provided ample evidence to support a finding of an intent to monopolize — to keep the American aluminum market Alcoa's exclusive preserve by whatever methods were required.

The district court's view of the law was that proof of a specific intent to monopolize was necessary to convict Alcoa. The trial judge found not illegal intent but merely prudent business motivations in Alcoa's accumulation and exercise of the competitive advantages that flowed from its vertical integration. Judge Hand did not reverse this finding as "clearly erroneous," except to hold that the price squeeze on rolling mills was prima facie evidence of illegal intent. Even the price squeeze, however, did not necessarily evince a specific intent to injure or to exclude, since it represented, in part, a means of probing the opportunities for increasing the use of aluminum sheet in competition with other metals — a kind of promotional price discrimination. An economist might reasonably contend that an inquiry into Alcoa's intent was not worthwhile. Alcoa's vertical integration imposed severe and entirely strategic handicaps upon non-integrated competitors, and erected substantial barriers against competitive entry.[9] The fact of market power alone, it might reasonably be argued, was significant. Given the market structure in aluminum, perhaps the vertical integration itself should have been held objectionable.

However, it was not necessary for the law to go to either extreme: condemning Alcoa's vertical integration per se, or condemning it contingent upon a demonstration of predatory intent. The decision could have hinged on the traditional test of monopolization, the evidence

[9] Compare Adelman's analysis: "The vice of integration, therefore, is its superior efficiency, for that makes it impossible for nonintegrated concerns to be 'able to compete.'" Adelman, "Integration and Antitrust Policy," 63 *Harv. L. Rev.* 27, 53 (1949).

of what the defendant *did*. Alcoa had the power to exclude. It maintained the power in part at least by methods other than those of normal competition. It *exercised* the power, with the result that actual and potential competitors were seriously squeezed. Because exclusion was the consequence not merely of its market power and structure but of its policies, an intent to monopolize might reasonably have been inferred. The test of intent is not a test of the purity of a company's motives, but an evaluation of its conduct. A company in Alcoa's position in ingot cannot be permitted to reduce prices *selectively* in such a way as to wipe out the profit margins of those who must buy from it as well as sell in competition with it. Nor can it be permitted, without limit, to extend its monopoly by such means as Alcoa employed.

Alcoa and the Requirements of Workable Competition

In determining whether or not the *Alcoa* decision violated the requirements of workable competition, the market performance of the industry, under the competitive stimulus of scrap, imports, and other metals, must be examined. While it is impossible to assess the complicated record with any pretension to scientific accuracy, Alcoa must unquestionably receive substantial credit for the rapid growth of the American aluminum industry, for the dramatic secular decline in prices and costs, and the corresponding expansion of capacity and in the uses of aluminum. But it is certainly doubtful that a complete monopoly of American ingot production was a necessary condition of this development. Economies of large-scale operation in production and research did not require a single producer. Moreover, one cautious and diffident appraisal concluded that the single seller was responsible for some substantial restriction of output and investment and that an oligopoly would probably have done better. . . . Moreover, the successful demand for an increase in the protective duty in 1922 (from 2c to 5c per lb., at which level it remained until 1930), and the prompt elevation of the price by the same amount, were surely evidence of unworkable competition. Alcoa's high profits, particularly in the monopoly ingot field, are further evidence. Average overall annual returns of 9.63% on stockholders' equity during the decade of the 1930's, 16.61% in 1935–39, and 27% in 1939 alone, would appear to vindicate the "dubious economics" of Judge Hand. Both economics and law appear to agree, then, that the *Alcoa* decision was correct in giving the Government the right to lay its hands on the aluminum industry.

The New Market Structure and Prospects of Better Performance

The decree in *Alcoa* and the Government's disposal of surplus World War II plants to Reynolds and Kaiser have substantially altered the market structure of the aluminum industry. There are now three large, vertically integrated domestic producers of aluminum, instead of one. And there is a huge potential competitor in Canada, enjoying unusually low costs, which will in time have no ties to Alcoa. The American producers enjoy rights under Alcoa's patents, and have been freed of the obligation to license that company under any patents which they may develop in the future. . . .

The only supportable economic criticism of *Alcoa* is not that the decree went too far, but that it did not go far enough. Competition in aluminum fabrication is still burdened by the industry's tight vertical integration. The introduction of two vertically integrated domestic producers has not greatly increased the availability of ingot to independent fabricators; the latter continue to be dependent upon their integrated competitors. The difficulties of the 17,000 independent fabricators during the recent defense program add appeal to the suggestion that Alcoa's fabrication and reduction facilities be separated.

The courts need not hesitate in splitting Alcoa along horizontal lines in 1954 merely because vertical integration has enabled the company in the past to press forward the development of sources of raw material and power, and new fabricating uses of aluminum. It might be possible to preserve the dynamic contributions of vertical integration, and still dilute Alcoa's power and increase the competitive opportunities of non-integrated fabricators. For example, all or part of Alcoa's *present* fabrication activities could be split off, while permitting the company to develop whatever *new* market outlets it chooses. Vertical integration is a threat to competition only where competition is seriously imperfect in one of the interconnected horizontal strata. In aluminum, the evil was Alcoa's monopoly of ingot. To the extent that this monopoly can be further dissipated, vertical integration, with its possible contributions to efficiency and innovation, may be safely left undisturbed.

Unless integrated firms so clearly abuse the power conferred by control of scarce materials that antitrust divestiture is justified, Government intervention outside of the antitrust laws is probably the only possible way of attempting to assure fairness in the distribution of such materials. . . .

"MONOPOLIZING" AS POSSESSION OF THE POWER TO EXCLUDE

The Cigarette and Movie Decisions

The *American Tobacco* decision strengthened the "new" Sherman Act's flat prohibition of monopoly power. The Supreme Court upheld a finding of conspiracy among three separate companies to fix prices and to monopolize, even though the record contained no direct evidence of collusion. Also, the mere joint possession by the "Big 3" in the tobacco industry of the power to exclude, accompanied by a conspiratorial intent to use it, was declared illegal; evidence of actual exclusion of competitors was unnecessary. There is strong reason to believe that the rigid and non-competitive price leadership practiced by the "Big 3" required no collusion, but followed naturally from an independent and rational pursuit of individual, oligopolistic interests. *American Tobacco* seemed, therefore, to go far in bringing normal oligopoly behavior, hence oligopoly itself, within the compass of the antitrust laws.[10]

This development was extended in the movie decisions of 1948. In the *Griffith* case, the chain embraced theaters in both one-theater and multi-theater towns, and bargained with distributors for exhibition rights in all theaters as a group. Griffith used the leverage of local monopolies in one-theater towns, where the distributor had to offer his pictures to Griffith if he was to have an audience at all, to obtain vital competitive advantages in the other towns. Among the valuable privileges obtained in this fashion were the rights of pre-emption in selecting films and long clearances over competitors. The Supreme Court held that such a situation conferred monopoly power; and, citing the *Alcoa* doctrine that "no monopolist monopolizes unconscious of what he is doing," it found, in the ways in which the chain bargained, abuse of that power sufficient to meet the test of the *Tobacco* case. Thus, the Court came close to condemning, per se, integration embracing a monopoly market. The situation need only confer a strategic advantage over competitors, and the leverage need only be employed. Integration almost inevitably confers such an advantage over non-integrated competitors in one or another of the markets in which the integrated firm operates.[11]

10 See Nicholls, *Price Policies in the Cigarette Industry* 172–86, 352–403 (1951). Some commentators have also found in *American Tobacco* a forthright condemnation of non-collusive power to fix prices, but this interpretation is unjustified. See Kahn, *supra* note 5, at 31–2.

11 See Kahn, *supra* note 5, at 43–6; Rostow, "Problems of Size and Integration" in *Business Practices under Federal Antitrust Laws* 122 (1952) (hereinafter cited as 1951 Symposium 3.

In the *Paramount* case, as in *Alcoa* and *Griffith,* the court of final jurisdiction was forced to resort to market structure arguments in the face of certain negative findings of fact by the district court. The district court had found that the five major producers had neither enjoyed nor sought, individually or collectively, a "national monopoly in exhibition." The Supreme Court focused, instead, on the market that the "Big 5" unquestionably monopolized – the first run field or "cream of the exhibition business" – and on the inherent advantages in access to first runs enjoyed by the exhibition houses of the vertically integrated producers. The Court followed the *Griffith* doctrine that a "specific intent" to monopolize need not be proven "if monopoly results as a necessary consequence of what was done." It therefore set aside the lower court's exculpation of the defendants, and granted the divestiture remedy.

Although the cigarette and movie decisions unquestionably strengthened the antitrust laws, their novelty has been exaggerated. First, strong circumstantial evidence indicated that the defendants in *American Tobacco* and *Paramount* had in effect agreed to eradicate price competition among themselves. Apart from the absence of direct evidence, the decisions on this score represented no advance over *Trenton Potteries* or *Socony-Vacuum.* Second, the *Tobacco* decision did not authorize attacks on the unexercised power to exclude. The Court said the Government had to prove that the companies had conspired to obtain and maintain the power to exclude competitors *and* had demonstrated an intent to use it. Since such an intent can be shown only by actual abuse of the power, the Court summarized the evidence of the exclusive tactics of the cigarette companies, which established the requisite intent to drive out competitors.

The movie cases of 1948 were even more replete with extreme competitive disadvantages imposed upon independents not only by the structure but also by the *actions* of the defendants. In *Paramount,* the Court held the five vertically integrated producers guilty of collaborative monopolization on the basis of a lengthy record of unreasonable clearances, pooling agreements, formula deals, master agreements, block booking, and discrimination, all at the expense of unaffiliated theaters. In *Griffith,* it found monopsony power exerted to obtain unfair competitive advantages, at the expense of exhibitors whose deficiency was one of bargaining power only. It did not strike at business arrangements that have the merely incidental consequence of excluding competitors from some area of the market. It rejected the Government's claim that vertical integration in the motion picture industry was inherently objectionable. The inescapable monopoly power of a movie house in a one-theater town was held not in itself to violate the law.[12] Power over price was condemned only if it was the product of collusion, and the power to exclude only after a showing that the defendants had actually exerted it.

The evil in both cigarettes and movies, then, was market power manifested in so clearly non-competitive a pattern of pricing as strongly to suggest conspiracy; vertical integration so clearly manifesting a struggle for monopolistic advantage, and market leverage so flagrantly *exerted* to impose unreasonable injury on competitors, as to justify condemnation for monopolizing.

The Economics of the Cigarette and Movie Decisions

A convincing argument can surely be made, with respect to both the *Tobacco* and *Paramount* cases, that the oligopolistic character of the markets together with the commanding power and strategic advantages of the defendants, were the appropriate grounds for the suit and should have sufficed to convict. In the cigarette industry, this market structure produced results about which no economist seems to have anything good to say. In movies, the severe imperfections of competition in both production and exhibition, resulting from fewness of sellers, the uniqueness of each product, and the monopoly power issuing from favorable location of theaters, suggest a particular threat to competition in permitting oligopolists to operate at both levels. In these circumstances, vertical integration inevitably reinforced the monopoly elements by increasing the impediments to entry at both levels, and engendered the rigidly channelized, essentially cooperative kind of competition that prevailed between the majors.

Even in these cases, however, it would have been dangerous to condemn the defendants merely because they were few, or few and vertically integrated, or enjoyed monopoly power. Their small number might have mirrored the survival of the fittest, the economies of scale, and the limitations of the market. As for condemning vertical integration per se, this form of business integration undoubtedly made a dynamic contribution. The leading producers had a particular incentive to make huge investments in the construction of new theaters, equipped for "talkies"; they wanted the widest possible audience for their films. They claimed that the resultant assurance of wide

[12] *See* United States v. Griffith, 334 U.S. 100, 106 (1948). Compare this dictum with Adelman's statement, in support of which he cites this same case: "It is now established doctrine that 'unreasonable' control over any local market, or any significant area of interstate commerce, is illegal." Adelman, "Integration and Antitrust Policy," 63 *Harv. L. Rev.* 27, 48 (1949).

distribution and exhibition in turn justified the heavy investments required to produce modern "A" films.

And in the movie cases, at least, it would have been equally undesirable to try to evaluate economic performance. A court should not be asked to decide, in an antitrust proceeding against movie companies, whether or not the quality and price of the extraordinarily variegated composite service in question, or the past or prospective contributions to that record of the particular restraints at issue, merit condemnation. Nor, as it would have to do in appraising the price record of the industry, should any Government agency decide whether or not the "stars" or motion picture executives deserve their extraordinary salaries and bonuses.

Although it is extremely difficult to predict the impact of the cigarette and movie decisions on the economic performance of the industries concerned, the change is certainly for the better. To the extent that the movie decrees are effective in improving the competitive opportunities of independent producers and exhibitors, they can only contribute at both levels to a greater ease of entry, which is the prime requisite of workable competition. The divorce of production and exhibition should make it more difficult for the producers to avoid price competition down the line. Breaking up the big theater chains may diminish their "countervailing power," and so incur the censure of Professor Galbraith, but there is no evidence that the chains used this power in any other way than to get monopolistic preferences for themselves. The cigarette companies, on the other hand, have only the implicit injunction not to do those imprecisely identifiable things which caused the jury to find them guilty. Yet even such a rule may be to some extent salutary. The conviction has apparently helped to engender a more moderate pricing policy. If the "Big 3" cannot be forced to compete, at least they can be discouraged from extortionate pricing under rigid price leadership.

The major impediments to entry and effective competition in cigarettes are not the threat of exclusionary tactics—about which the "Big 3" will presumably be more circumspect in the future—but rather the immense cost of advertising, consumer acceptance of the familiar brands, and the regressive federal excise tax. The antitrust laws alone cannot eradicate all these influences. But they can do much even here. The Supreme Court has already taken cognizance of the fact that heavy advertising expenditures represent a substantial bulwark of the "Big 3's" monopoly power. In line with past decrees requiring compulsory licensing in patent cases, and condemning otherwise legal practices and relationships when power has been abused, a decree which limited advertising expenditures of each of the "Big 3" to a certain percentage of gross revenues would seem feasible. If economists agree on anything, they probably agree that in cigarettes a limitation of advertising would offer some hope for freer entry and bona fide competition of a socially useful kind.

"MONOPOLIZING" WITHOUT ACHIEVING MONOPOLY

After *Alcoa,* "new" Sherman Act decisions went further than merely bringing the law nearer to a position of outlawing monopoly power as such. They suggested the possibility of condemning companies for controlling some appreciable portion of interstate commerce. This conception of monopolizing was much more disturbing to economists than the one in *Alcoa,* because the "any part" of commerce which might be "monopolized" was not defined in economically realistic terms. Consequently, a company might be held to have monopolized without ever having achieved significant monopoly power.

The *A & P* decision condemned a company that had helped to introduce strong competition into the distribution of grocery products. The conviction hinged essentially on abuses of power, in the traditional sense. *A & P* thus represents an extension of the logic of the movie decisions. In both, the defendants enjoyed a strategic superiority over their competitors, by virtue of their size, bargaining power, and vertical integration, as well as the geographic dispersion of their operations. And, as in the movie decisions, the existence of power was combined with some evidence of an intent to exercise it. A & P coercively bargained for discriminatory discounts, and operated on unusually low retail margins in selected market areas to "put the heat on" competitors.[13]

But in the absence of anything approaching convincing evidence of undesirable market consequences, the *A & P* opinions also demonstrate *some* tendency to attack the quest for bargains and discounts justified by the performance of functions; efficient vertical integration on the ground that the profits earned therefrom illegally subsidized retail competition; any regional discrepancies in margins maintained by a big and powerful company, whether promotional, defensive, or predatory in nature.

A similar disregard for the overall market consequences of an integrated firm's strategic competitive advantages was suggested in the

[13] See the exchange between Dirlam & Kahn and Adelman, in 61 *J. Pol. Econ.* 436 (1953).

first *Yellow Cab* case.[14] In *Yellow Cab* the Supreme Court held that *if* the evidence demonstrated an intent to monopolize, the mere fact that the vertical integration of taxicab manufacturing and operating companies precluded competitor manufacturers from a substantial market would be sufficient to condemn the arrangement under Section 2 of the Sherman Act. Taxicabs are sold in a nation-wide market, and only a very small portion of that market was affected by the defendant's activities, particularly since most taxicabs are nothing more than specially painted passenger cars. By defining "any part" of interstate commerce as nothing more than a *volume of business* large enough to satisfy a *de minimis* requirement, and by extending the doctrine of conspiracy to the organizers of a proprietary consolidation, the Court in effect condemned all vertical integration, contingent on the necessary demonstration of intent to monopolize. However, subsequent proceedings have shown that the latter condition is truly a substantial one.

Similarly the *International Salt* case in effect found any patent tie-in a violation of both Section 1 of the Sherman Act and Section 3 of the Clayton Act, without regard to whether or not it substantially reduced competition in the tied-in field as a whole. After declaring that "it is unreasonable, *per se,* to foreclose competitors from any substantial market," the Supreme Court inferred a sufficient effect on competition from the mere fact that "the volume of business affected by these contracts cannot be said to be insignificant or insubstantial and the tendency of the arrangement to accomplishment of monopoly seems obvious. . . ." The "any part" of interstate commerce deemed sufficient in *Yellow Cab* to condemn vertical integration which was improperly motivated is obviously the same thing as the not insignificant volume of business from which patent tie-ins may no longer legally foreclose competitors.

It was the later extension of the reasoning in *International Salt* to exclusive dealing, and the apparently ominous implications of *Yellow Cab* for vertical integration achieved by financial consolidation, which make these two opinions significant.

Exclusive Dealing and Full Requirements Contracts

A realistic policy of maintaining competition must be flexible. It must leave room within limits for price discrimination, exclusive dealing

14 United States v. Yellow Cab Co., 332 U.S. 218 (1947). For a discussion of this and other intra-enterprise conspiracy cases, see Comment, 63 *Yale L.J.* 372 (1954).

and full requirements contracts, tie-ins and package deals. Yet, it must prevent the *unfair* or *excessive* constriction of market opportunities of competitors that these practices may entail.[15] Striking the balance between these offsetting considerations has been the historic purpose and function of the rule of reason, embodied not only in the courts' interpretations of the Sherman Act but also in the Clayton Act which restricts its prohibitions to instances where competition is threatened.

The *A & P, International Salt* and first *Yellow Cab* decisions, though involving dissimilar business structures and practices had this in common: they suggested that the Sherman Act condemns any of the above-mentioned practices if they represent the use of market leverage or financial resources to put competitors at a disadvantage, regardless of any other economic consequences.

Recent Clayton Act decisions have shown the same tendency. At the risk of some oversimplification, it may be said that Sections 2 and 3 of the Clayton Act were for many years interpreted to require a demonstration that the practices would *probably* have the effect of weakening the force of competition in the *entire interstate* market affected; and that recent decisions have tended to reduce the requirement to a showing that the practices may *possibly* weaken the forces of competition, now or in the future, in some *not insubstantial portion* of the market, sectional or national, but putting *some competitors* of the defendant, or his customers, at a disadvantage. The modern view clearly comes much closer to, indeed may be tantamount to, outlawing the specified practices per se, which would mean the adoption of pure competition as the law's standard.

Standard Oil Co. v. United States (*Standard Stations*) is the most important recent case under Section 3 of the Clayton Act. Assessment of the competitive impact of Standard's full requirements contracts was the primary issue. In contrast with the previous decisions, the Supreme Court in this case set out to require the Government to assume the burden of "some sort of showing as to the *actual* or *probable economic consequences of* the agreements. . . ."[16] How-

[15] The basic question before us is whether it would suffice to delete the words "unfair or" from this sentence. The "new critics" of antitrust favor deletion, since they would have us judge these practices mainly, if not entirely, by appraising their overall consequences. My view is that "unfair or" should be retained, since the act of exclusion, properly defined as an act to unfairly preclude competitive entry, should itself be prohibited.

[16] Standard Oil Co. v. United States, 337 U.S. 293, 302 (1949) (emphasis added).

ever, it found "the qualifying clause of § 3 . . . satisfied by proof that competition has been foreclosed in a substantial share of the line of commerce affected." The satisfying "proof" was the demonstration that Standard's full requirements contracts covered 16% of the retail gasoline outlets and 6.7% of the total gasoline sales in the western states. The substantiality of Standard's percentage share of the market was certainly a more significant evidence of competitive impact than sufficed in *International Salt*. But still, the Court really declined to appraise the economic consequences, to consider whether or not the requirements contracts were economically beneficial, or intensified rather than reduced competition in the market. In short, *Standard Stations* seemed to say that all full requirements contracts covering any "substantial" share of commerce are *ipso facto* illegal because by their very nature they exclude competitors from that segment of trade which they cover.

The *Richfield* decision merely extended *Standard Stations'* prohibition to another member of the petroleum industry's "Big 7" on the West Coast. The main formal difference between the two cases concerned Richfield's defense of its contracts with the 1,343 dealers (about 45 percent of the total) who were its own lessees. These, it contended, were not independent businessmen, but, in effect, its employees; it had "created" their businesses and could therefore hardly be suppressing pre-existing competition in confining their sales to its own products. The district court dismissed this argument on the ground that by all the traditional tests the lessees were independent businessmen who assumed all the usual responsibilities and risks.

In appraising these developments, we will have two major questions to ask. First, how much of the rule of reason is left? Second, can the attenuated rule of reason that remains still play its historic economic role in modern markets, where pure competition is neither attainable nor desirable? The discussion will relate mainly to tie-ins, exclusive dealing, and requirements contracts, though much of it applies to price discrimination as well.

The law does not turn on the incidental exclusion of competitors effected by contracts issuing from a process of fair competition. Legality depends on whether or not power has been *exerted* in such a way as to impose an unreasonable handicap on competitors. Condemnation requires, in short, something like an intent to monopolize, carried into effect. Only if the requisite power and intent are present, *i.e.*, if the objectionable character of the action is established, does the law strike down arrangements, contractual or proprietary, which do no more than exclude competitors from a "not insubstantial" market. Admittedly, however, the leading cases do not say this clearly.

* * *

EXCLUSIVE DEALING IN OIL AND EFFECTIVE COMPETITION

In *Standard Stations,* the Court prudently refused to apply economic performance tests. It chose to ignore the fact that exclusive dealing is "a device for waging competition," as well as for denying competitors access to the market, and that "retail stations . . . are the instrumentalities through which competition for . . . [the] ultimate market is waged."[17] It is not at all clear that the dominant companies were progressively able to entrench themselves through exclusive dealing, or to eliminate competition among themselves. Numerous elements of intense and socially beneficial competition exist in the rivalry among majors and independents *for* dealers and retail outlets, and *through* dealers for consumer patronage. It is unlikely that the major oil companies or any one else would have constructed so many conveniently situated service stations had not the refiners some assurance that the stations would carry their own products exclusively, or that, without the exclusive link, the refiner could so successfully have induced dealers to maintain clean rest rooms and provide the motorist with many other services. Oil companies have constructed their own exclusive outlets in order to compete more effectively in the final market with refiners and distributors already entrenched in that market. And exclusive dealing has often helped to assure adequate representation for the producer of an unknown brand.

On the other hand, exclusive dealing has detrimental effects on workable competition. Competition by pre-emption of desirable sites and market outlets has probably produced an uneconomic profusion of service stations. Moreover, competition through tied outlets is competition of a channelized and limited kind. Control over these outlets confers on the big refiner a means of limiting price rivalry at both retail and wholesale levels, and of impeding access to the market by the smaller, independent refiners and marketers, who are usually the price cutters. Standard of California has been the price leader on the West Coast and a price cutter in the East largely because in the one it enjoys, and in the other it lacks, a broad market coverage with controlled outlets.

[17] Standard Oil Co. v. United States, 337 U.S. 293, 321–4 (1949) (dissenting opinion).

Moreover, it is difficult to see why many of the mutual benefits and socially beneficent consequences of exclusive dealing require coercion for their achievement. Nothing prevents refiners from granting discounts that measure the cost savings of regularly scheduled, volume purchases. There is no reason why a supplier could not continue to give advice, assistance, and free paint to dealers who handle its products, as long as these favors are not conditioned on exclusive handling, and still exert pressure on dealers to keep their rest rooms clean, wipe windshields, and provide free air. In any case, now that the motorist has become accustomed to these free services, the keen competition among dealers should ensure that they will continue to be forthcoming.

An economist can hardly be certain that a law which denies to dominant refiners the right to insist on exclusive dealing will weaken the force of market competition. The probabilities would seem to be to the contrary, and this is, after all, what the Clayton Act presumed and *Standard Stations* contends. It is not necessarily an undesirable consequence of *Standard Stations* that a major refiner wishing to exercise firmer control over retail outlets than the law now permits must assume the additional risks and responsibilities of owning and operating them itself. That full integration may permit greater operating control is balanced by the fact that it is also more expensive. In the face of social security and chain store taxes, it seems unlikely that the oil companies will attempt full integration.

* * *

The apparent willingness of the courts to permit exclusive supply arrangements which are not the product of coercion, and which are beneficial to both parties without unreasonably excluding competitors, suggests that the earlier *Bausch & Lomb*[18] decision still stands. This case involved a contract between Bausch & Lomb, which manufactured and ground pink-tinted lenses, and the Soft-Lite Lens Co., the exclusive distributor, which sold the lenses under its trade name. These arrangements were held legal, because they "were developed through arm's length negotiations," and protected Soft-Lite, which was "spending large sums to develop [its] good will and enlarge the public patronage of a relatively new article of commerce." Moreover, Bausch & Lomb did not have a monopoly in the manufacture of glass for lenses. "On the contrary . . . other manufacturers of lenses have

[18] United States v. Bausch & Lomb Optical Co., 45 F. Supp. 387 (S.D.N.Y.) 1942), *aff'd.* 321 U.S. 707 (1944).

had access to pink glasses from other sources and . . . the success of Soft-Lite . . . stimulated emulation and competition." Furthermore, "there [was] competition between untinted and tinted lenses, as well as in the various tints of lenses and among the distributors of pink tinted lenses. . . ." In short, the agreement did not involve the use of market power by a dominant seller to exclude competitors. It was not anti-competitive either in intent or in effect.

* * *

J. I. Case

The recent antitrust suit against J. I. Case[19] illustrates how complex the task often is of drawing the line between competition and exclusion. Most farm machinery is sold through dealers, each of whom is the exclusive local representative of a single full-line manufacturer, and for the most part handles the line of only one manufacturer. The exclusiveness is not tight, since only a small minority of dealers handle no competitive equipment whatsoever. Although these arrangements are not embodied in binding contracts, the exclusive agency-exclusive dealing pattern is typical, particularly as far as the full line is concerned. To break up this pattern, the Department of Justice launched civil suits against International Harvester, John Deere and J. I. Case; when it lost the suit against Case in the district court, the only one to go to trial, it dropped them all.

The Government contended that it was the general policy of J. I. Case to have its dealers handle its products exclusively. The district court agreed "that Case has been intent . . . on obtaining dealers who will devote the major part of their activities to the Case line. . . ." The Government also argued that the company's field representatives continually exerted pressure on the retailers, backed by the threat of contract termination, to drop competitive lines. It cited 108 dealers as having been subjected to specific acts of coercion and pressure of this kind. The court conceded that there had been "flagrant attempts to coerce and put pressure on a few dealers to give up competing lines as a condition for obtaining a Case contract or to obtain a renewal. . . ." These policies and pressures, the Government contended, had caused contracts with a substantial and increasing number of dealers to be accompanied by understandings that they would be exclusive, and therefore effected an unreasonable restraint of trade under Section 1 of the Sherman Act. These understandings also violated Section 3 of the Clayton Act, it argued, regardless of

[19] United States v. J. I. Case Co., 101 F. Supp. 856 (D. Minn. 1951).

whether they were secured by coercion, since the effect was to exclude competitors from selling to large numbers of the Case dealership organization. In short, the Government contended that the market must be free of even voluntary contractual constraints; at every moment everyone must be free to contract with everyone else.

The court, on the other hand, saw no legal objection to exclusive dealing as such, whether secured by contract or understanding. The manufacturers had the right to select distributors according to whether or not they gave its products "fair representation," and were "sold, so to speak, and enthusiastic about its line." And, the manufacturer might reasonably withdraw its machines from a dealer who divided his loyalties and attention between two full lines. But, the purpose of these methods must not be to effect a monopoly, and the methods cannot be "unreasonably coercive." Moreover, there must be little likelihood that the intensity of competition in the final market will be diminished.

The court found that Case's actions fell within these rather vague boundaries of legitimacy. Company bulletins advised sales personnel not to be "over-zealous," to avoid "dictating" to or "coercing" dealers with respect to the lines they carried, while at the same time assuring the personnel that they could insist on adequate representation of the company's line. The court attributed exclusive handling of Case's products not to pressure by the manufacturer, but to a mutual recognition that sound business practice demanded it, and held that arrangements thus arrived at are legal.

The court held that Case's policies had no substantial deleterious effect on competition, actual or potential. Over 70% of Case's dealers carried competitive products, though few carried another full line. There was no testimony from competing manufacturers that exclusive dealing had excluded them from markets. On the contrary, the court found that most towns had dealers representing nearly every full-line and many short-line manufacturers. It found, in short, that workable competition prevailed.

The opinion in *J. I. Case* was an accurate interpretation of the law. Exclusive dealing in farm equipment cannot be illegal per se. On the other hand, there is force in the Government's contention that the record may have justified an equity decree to redress a market situation characterized by inequalities of competitive access, and of bargaining power between supplier and dealer. It is impossible to characterize such inequality with any precision. Manufacturers depend heavily on their dealers, who are their only direct contact with the final customer. A good dealer can therefore offer considerable resistance to what he considers unjustified demands by a supplier, and dealers have often been able to shift from one supplier to another. This opportunity has been enhanced by the entry of new full-line companies like Ford and Ferguson. A big company, however, can get along without a particular dealer, and the number of full-line companies is very limited. The right to handle the line of one of these companies may mean the dealer's entire livelihood, and be sufficiently precious to induce him to succumb to the supplier's pressure to do things that are not necessarily in his or the public's interest.

In these circumstances, the fact that buyers and sellers find exclusive contractual relationships sufficiently satisfactory to enter into them does not necessarily make them socially acceptable. The existence of mutual economic advantages in such an arrangement does not justify a seller's *insisting* on it. The presumption in antitrust law must be against exclusive tactics, and in favor of easier entry into oligopolistic markets. The structure of the farm machinery industry is not greatly different from that of the west coast petroleum industry. Since the policies of all the farm machinery leaders paralleled those of Case, the court might well have found in this case, as the Supreme Court did in *Standard Stations,* that exclusive dealing policies illegally perpetuated a pattern of oligopoly. The important difference between the two cases is that in *Standard Stations* exclusive dealing was the clearly established practice and openly avowed policy of the defendant, and in *Case* the practice was far looser. None the less, a decree prohibiting coercive pressure for exclusive dealing might have forced Case to be more scrupulous in keeping its field representatives from overstepping the bounds of reasonable salesmanship.

The antitrust laws have traditionally condemned certain kinds of business behavior; they do not attack market situations or business arrangements. Accordingly, the legal appraisal of full requirements contracts must turn on whether or not they issue from the *exertion* of market or financial power, with the effect of constructing substantial impediments to competitive entry. The more flagrant the exclusive tactics, the more clearly they betray an intent to exclude, the less stringent should be the test of market consequences. The prime question is whether the act of exclusion is unreasonable, or stems merely from socially acceptable methods of vying for customer patronage, and from the free decision of the dealer or buyer. These are the traditional tests of the rule of reason, and they probably still apply. . . .

The cases show the impracticality of drawing the line between reasonable and unreasonable restraints on the basis of purely economic judgments of industrial performance. Whether the economist would agree with the court in *J. I. Case* that competition is effective in farm machinery would depend on the economist. The same is true in petroleum. One must concede that an unhampered insistence on exclusive dealing or full requirements contracts by J. I. Case, Standard of California or American Can would be most unlikely in itself to increase substantially their respective market shares. Nor would sweeping antitrust condemnations of exclusive arrangements radically change either the competitive methods or the economic performance of the farm machinery, petroleum and can industries. Yet, it is reasonable to conclude that a pattern of oligopoly control of markets may be indefinitely extended, and entry continually hampered, by the insistence of all the dominant producers on this marketing practice. Against the benefit to the consumer because a big manufacturer can plan more effectively and can hold retailers to higher levels of performance under exclusive systems of marketing, must be weighed the consumer's interest in the widest possible range of choice among manufacturers and in being served by retailers sufficiently expert and *free* to help him choose the particular products that best meet his particular needs. Although some commentators imply that a blanket prohibition of the use of power to exclude competitors from "a substantial market" may "indiscriminately strike down the good with the bad," the seriousness of the risk has yet to be demonstrated.

Vertical Integration—Persistence of the Double Standard

There has always been a double standard in the antitrust laws. Restrictive agreements between separate firms are more severely treated than proprietary consolidations enjoying just as great or greater market power. The double standard appeared in the contrasting treatment accorded the first two groups of business defendants whose cases reached the Supreme Court—one involving a merger, the other a price-fixing conspiracy.[20] The decision which finally established that the law could reach mergers in industry[21] at the same time set forth the rule of reason, which, subsequent decisions demonstrated, re-

[20] *Compare* United States v. E. C. Knight Co., 156 U.S. 1 (1895), *with* United States v. Trans-Missouri Freight Ass'n, 166 U.S. 290 (1897).

[21] Standard Oil Co. v. United States, 221 U.S. 1 (1911).

established the double standard in another form. A big firm, however powerful, had to misbehave to fall afoul of the law; a price-fixing or market-sharing agreement among separate firms, though covering no greater a share of the market than the single firm, was illegal per se. Judge Hand's decision in *Alcoa* was the first instance in which a court of final jurisdiction explicitly rejected this dual approach; the evil, he said, was monopoly power, in whatever form. But this vigorous attack on monopoly power per se was limited to true "monopolies" in the classic sense. And the subsequent cigarette and movie cases hinged not merely on the market power conveyed by size and integration, but on the *intent* to exclude competitors.

Probably no single case has been more responsible than the criminal and civil suits against A & P for the widespread but erroneous impression that the law now condemns integration and size. Admittedly, the courts inadequately differentiated the economically beneficial and legally "reasonable" from the undesirable and unreasonable aspects of A & P's organization and tactics and their consequences. However, even a hasty perusal of the district court's opinion should satisfy any fair reader that the impression is essentially an illusion. To be sure, A & P would probably have escaped antitrust prosecution had it not also been large, integrated, and aggressive. But it was not convicted on these grounds. According to the court, the Government had contended, and would have to prove "that the size of A & P, its integration . . . were so *employed* as to bring about inevitably unreasonable advantages. . . . The charge is that defendants have so *utilized* their power and integration as unreasonably to restrain commerce."[22] Certainly this is what the court thought the Government had proved. The opinion is replete with clear-cut disavowals of hostility to size and integration alone.

It seems impossible to doubt that the court conscientiously tried to apply a rule of reason in the *A & P* case, and to differentiate mere size and integration from abuse of the power that they conferred. The court's analysis of A & P's operations centered on the sources and uses of the company's "headquarters profits." Scattered references to the "subsidization" of retail operations by these "profits," particularly those referring to the "profits" from manufacturing, appear to betray a basic hostility toward vertical integration itself. But the discussion consists almost entirely of a demonstration that all but the "profits" from manufacturing were tainted in their source – being the product

[22] 67 F. Supp. 626, 642 (E.D. Ill. 1946) (emphasis added).

of coercive bargaining—and all were deliberately misused at the retail level.

According to the "new critics" of the Sherman Act, A & P would not have been condemned under the "old" rule of reason. Competition may be fostered by big buyers bargaining hard with suppliers or cutting retail margins, even if selectively. The antitrust laws did not interfere with this impure yet competitive market behavior as long as the rule of reason took into consideration the market results, and not merely the unfair disadvantaging of smaller competitors. There was no evidence that A & P had achieved any substantial monopoly power, or that its retail and bargaining tactics had seriously jeopardized competition in the retail grocery business. It is therefore difficult to construct a positive defense of the A & P decision in purely economic terms. Nevertheless, in terms of the values of a free enterprise system, many of the company's actions were indefensible. A & P may not have enjoyed substantial monopoly power in most of its markets; yet in some, where it controlled a very large share, it must have had some such power; and it unquestionably enjoyed and abused certain kinds of "power."

The appropriate question, then, is whether or not the *A & P* case has brought to light a conflict between the requirements of workable competition and the mores of a free enterprise system. The conflict is not a serious one. The contributions to superior economic performance by those activities of A & P which are now clearly illegal were relatively unimportant when compared with the legitimate contributions of its integrated organization and operations. Against the possible contributions to workable competition by A & P's pressure on suppliers for discriminatory preferences and its selective local price cutting must be weighed the exploitation of weaker suppliers, and the discouragement to new entrants and to retail competition posed by discriminatory sharpshooting designed to demonstrate to the grocery that dares to open in an A & P town "that they have no place in the supermarket business in Richmond." The industry's performance is likely to improve rather than suffer if A & P is broken up in order to reduce its power to engage in unfair competition. As in the retailing of gasoline, so in groceries, the large-volume, low-margin outlet was an innovation of local independents, not the great chains. To the extent that grocery chains are denied recourse to price discrimination and to the resources of parents and affiliates, the opportunities for such independent entry are enhanced, and the chains themselves might be forced into more drastic and socially more beneficial adjustments to meet competition.

VERTICAL INTEGRATION AND "SPECIFIC" INTENT

The "new" Sherman Act, like the "old," condemns vertical integration only when it represents a device for extending monopoly power from one stratum to another. Very little is required in the way of a demonstration of market consequences, if a course of conduct may clearly be characterized as betraying such an intent to monopolize. On the other hand, if a course of conduct cannot be so clearly characterized, the "new" Sherman Act reserves its censure for actions or structures that threaten to impair the effectiveness of competition in the market regarded as a whole. Thus, in *Yellow Cab* the defendants' stock purchases did not reveal an intent to monopolize, and, since the impact on market competition was minimal, the Government eventually lost the case. Similarly in *Columbia Steel,* the Supreme Court established beyond all question that in the presence of legitimate business reasons for the acquisition of a customer, vertical integration is not invalid merely because it shuts competitors out of three percent of a market. However, the Court recognized that "legitimate" intent would not exonerate mergers with truly substantial overall market consequences, and therefore grappled conscientiously with the economic facts to see whether or not the defendant's acquisition would have "the effect . . . [of] unreasonably restrict[ing] the opportunities of competitors to market their product."

Columbia Steel was based on questionable findings of fact. In ascertaining the intent underlying the acquisition, the Court essentially accepted at face value U.S. Steel's contention that it had to control an outlet for its Geneva output. Moreover, in terms of the size, origin and already substantial power of U.S. Steel, and the pattern of limited competition that has for decades characterized the steel industry, the market consequences of the acquisition should have been apparent. However, the blessing which the Attorney General previously conferred on the disposal of the Geneva plant to U.S. Steel unfortunately confined the instant case to the narrower question of the legality of the one subsequent acquisition.

Given the limited issue, the Court might still have interpreted the facts differently. It might well have concluded that the social drawbacks of permitting the dominant steel company to *acquire* rather than to construct a controlled outlet more than offset "the legitimate business reasons" for choosing the former course. Certainly the Federal Trade Commission, in enforcing the amended Section 7 of the Clayton Act, should make precisely this kind of appraisal of the relative economic merits of mergers *versus* expansion by construction of new facilities.

The dissenters in the second *Yellow Cab* case would have relieved the Government of the necessity of demonstrating a "specific intent" to monopolize, and retained the attenuated requirement of competitive impact accepted in the *International Salt* and first *Yellow Cab* cases. They would have had the decision turn on whether or not "the freedom of the taxicab companies to buy taxicabs has been hobbled by the defendants' business arrangements. . . .[23] Since vertical integration by merger ordinarily "hobbles" the subsequent freedom of choice of the mergered firms, the dissenters apparently seek the complete abolition of the rule of reason applied to such acquisitions. However, a good case can be made for upholding the Government's complaint in *Yellow Cab,* even under the rule of reason. Here, as in *Columbia Steel,* we have the phenomenon of mergers for "ordinary business reasons" which may none the less be economically undesirable, even though it is difficult to prove a substantial resultant impairment of the force of competition in the market as a whole. The rule of reason does not preclude asking what socially beneficent considerations might justify a taxicab manufacturer's acquiring control of a number of operating companies, most of which held monopolies in their respective local markets. And if, as appears to have been the case here, the operating companies, after the transfer of financial control, began to buy the higher-priced cabs of the acquiring manufacturer exclusively, the economist may wonder whether the cab rider did not eventually pay higher prices; and the judge may well agree with the Government that the defendants had effected an unreasonable restraint by using vertical integration to extend the benefits of monopoly from one market to another.

THE INEVITABILITY OF A DOUBLE STANDARD

Restrictive agreements and the exertion of monopolistic leverage reveal a manifest intent to exclude or unfairly handicap competitors, which is not necessarily present in cases involving vertical integration. The *Griffith* case involved manifestly exclusive tactics; an integrated theater chain *used* its bargaining power and market leverage to obtain unfair advantages over competitors. What was true of the tactics of the Griffith chain was also true in a sense of the condemned activities or contracts in *Standard Stations, Richfield, American Can, International Salt,* and even *National City Lines.* The company policies producing these contractual provisions or understandings were exclusionary on their face. Moreover, the defendants could have achieved

[23] United States v. Yellow Cab Co., 338 U.S. 338, 343 (1949).

most of the economically legitimate benefits without the *imposition* of restrictive, exclusive clauses. Condemnation, therefore, required—and in *Times-Picayune* should have required—demonstration of a lesser degree of competitive impact than in the case of vertical integration. In *Columbia Steel* and *Yellow Cab,* on the other hand, any handicaps imposed on competitors were merely the incidental consequences of integration by merger. The intent underlying vertical integration by merger is seldom clearly exclusionary. It may have other, socially acceptable purposes and consequences. Only if market leverage is exerted to force the transaction, or, after the merger has occurred, to put competitors at an unreasonable disadvantage is a virtually per se condemnation, similar to that of restrictive agreements, either legally or economically justified. This is the inescapable double standard.

Critics of the *Columbia Steel* and second *Yellow Cab* decisions on the one hand, and of *Standard Stations* and *National City Lines* on the other, join in arguing that it is inconsistent to permit a firm to do by financial acquisition what it may not do by contract. The criticism has considerable force. It supports the logic of the recent amendment to Section 7 of the Clayton Act, or to proposed amendments which would condemn excessively monopolistic market structures.

But any attempt to apply to integration, even if by merger, the same treatment as the new Sherman Act applies to exclusive dealing imposed by a dominant firm ignores an essential element of a profit system. If a company is willing to assume the risks of ownership, it must be permitted a wider measure of control than where it is contracting with independent parties. Investment cannot be equated at law with coercion and exclusion. It would also be economically disastrous to deny to a big business the right to produce for its own needs or to do its own marketing; to utilize some by-product idea or material in a new field; or to enter some new market, perhaps, by acquiring a firm already there. Such integration is a prime source of economic progress, and effective competition. The achievement of such differential advantages by coercion of suppliers into discriminatory preferences, or of marketers or customers into exclusive arrangements, does not make a comparable contribution. . . .

CONCLUSION

The underlying assumption of our antitrust laws is that competition cannot long remain effective if it is not also regulated in such a way as to keep it a fair contest on the basis of efficiency in serving the public. The laws seek to preserve both fairness and effectiveness by prohibiting collusion, unreasonable agglomeration, the wielding of massed power, and exclusive practices which suppress or pervert the competitive process. It is doubtful that economics supplies any more effective criteria of unreasonable restraint or undesirable monopolization than these traditional legal concepts. The "new critics" of antitrust argue that it is possible for exclusive, coercive, or discriminatory contracts or actions to contribute to workable competition and economic progress. Although a plausible *a priori* case can be made for this contention, the economic evidence is by no means convincing. Attempts to demonstrate the beneficial consequences of discrimination and exclusive systems of distribution are usually confined to an exposition of their undeniably competitive aspects: the supplier is forced to reduce his price selectively to get the business; the manufacturer imposes exclusive dealing to cut costs or intensify his selling effort. On the other hand, opponents of such practices usually confine themselves to a demonstration of their anti-competitive aspects: the supplier maintains his price to less powerful or fortunately situated buyers; exclusive dealing excludes competitors. Both arguments are inadequate.

The conclusion drawn from the foregoing appraisal of leading antitrust cases of the last ten years is that the traditional presumption against exclusive tactics and systematic discrimination remains at the core of the law, and is a justified one. A free enterprise system cannot tolerate substantial and persistent disparities between reality and the ideal of a fair field and no favors. Inevitable differences in competitive strength and threats to free competition on the basis of efficiency are created by inequalities in access to capital, and by the inherent competitive advantages of size, established position, and integration. The "new" Sherman and Clayton Acts intervene only when these advantages and these threats are compounded through coercion, exclusion, and systematic discrimination; it would require more convincing demonstrations that these tactics are necessary for effective competition than have heretofore been offered, to prove that the economic theory of the "new" Sherman and Clayton Acts is unsound.

PART THREE

STRUCTURE OR PERFORMANCE?

INTRODUCTION

Professor Kaysen agrees basically with Rostow's interpretation of the meaning of the Section 1 cases. He considers that the Supreme Court will regard parallel action as illegal collusion without requiring explicit proof of the coordinating mechanism. He disagrees, however, on the adequacy of this criterion alone for establishing illegality, especially in tight-knit oligopoly situations. Introducing the notion of "the agreement to agree" as a natural result in a market of the few, Kaysen asserts that the basic question is one of structure. Concern with the absence or presence of parallel action diverts attention from those very structural elements which tend to inspire, if not enforce, common behavior. Behavior, in Kaysen's view, is a function of market structure. By implication, the solution to problems of monopoly must be structural—the Triple D: Divestment, Divestiture, and Divorcement.

Professor Heflebower, on the other hand, holds that performance is not uniquely determined by market structure. While admitting that indeed there may be degrees of power (size) "dangerous either by themselves" (absolute size) or "because they facilitate effective tacit collusion" (relative size), the major criterion for determining legality of action is and should be performance. He considers "gigantism" to be an irreversible fact of economic life. We should be concerned, he argues, not so much with size, but rather with actual performance, i.e., the workability of competition. Structural remedies, therefore, are for the most part ruled out.

CARL KAYSEN

Collusion under the Sherman Act*

THE notion of collusion among business rivals, in the sense of joint action to divide markets or fix prices, is a central one in the history of Sherman Act enforcement. Such collusive action is the substance of the "conspiracy in restraint of trade" which Section 1 of the act makes a crime. Of what might be called classic examples of collusion, the Addyston Pipe Case was one of the first of a line which includes, among others, the American Column and Lumber, Trenton Potteries, and Madison Oil cases. In each case the finding of collusion rested on ample evidence of elaborate machinery for maintaining communication among the members of the several conspiracies.

In several recent cases, notably the second Tobacco case and two basing point cases,[1] the courts have found collusion on the basis of a rather different kind of evidence. The operation of an illegal conspiracy was an important part of the offense charged in each of these cases. Yet proof of the existence of elaborate machinery of communication among the defendants was notably absent from the government arguments in the trials. Instead, there was emphasis on the existence of a "planned common course of action" in the words of the FTC, or the existence of "mutual understanding or agreement" in those of the majority of the Court.[2] The courts found proof of the

* Reprinted by permission of the publishers from Carl Kaysen, "Collusion under the Sherman Act," *Quarterly Journal of Economics,* No. 65 (1951), (Cambridge, Mass.: Harvard University Press). Copyright, 1951, by the President and Fellows of Harvard University.

[1] American Tobacco Co. et al v. U.S., 328 U.S. 781 (1946); FTC v. Cement Institute et al, 333 U.S. 683 (1948); Triangle Conduit and Cable Inc. v. FTC, 168 Fed 2d 175 (1948) and U.S. Although the Cement Institute and Rigid Steel Conduit cases were brought under the Federal Trade Commission Act, rather than under the Sherman Act, the allegation of an illegal conspiracy was an essential part of both cases.

[2] The Court's phrase appears in the Cement Institute decision, 333 U.S. at 797. The Commission's words are quoted in the same opinion.

plan or understanding in a common pattern of action in the market. Moreover, these patterns of action were held proof of underlying conspiracy in the face of pleas by the defendants that they were consistent with independent action by each enterprise, and, in fact, resulted from independent action on the part of each in response to the circumstances of the market.

These decisions have occasioned much comment, both hostile and sympathetic. Business reaction to the admission of parallel action in itself as evidence of collusion, especially as expressed in the basing point cases, has been nearly uniformly hostile. An example of a sympathetic view of the kind of evidence on which collusion was found in the Tobacco Case is provided in an analysis by Professor E. V. Rostow of the Yale Law School.[3] The result of the Tobacco case, he says, is that "parallel action based on acknowledged self-interest within a defined market structure is sufficient evidence of illegal action under Section 1 of the Sherman Act." Professor Rostow hails this change in the law as one which squares the doctrines of the law with the realities of economics, and thus makes the Sherman Act a fitter instrument of social control.

What are the realities of economics in this area? Or perhaps, it is better to ask more modestly, what light can economics shed on the legal problem of the kind of inferences which can be drawn from parallel action in the market with respect to the fundamental independence of decisions of the firms involved? Analysis of this problem can most conveniently begin with a market situation in which the "classic" notion of collusion cited above is appropriate. Consider an imperfectly competitive market in which there are a large number of sellers and buyers, none of dominant importance, and in which buyers always act independently of each other. Considerable elements of ignorance and uncertainty exist: sellers are not assumed to have complete knowledge of the demand curves for their outputs, nor even complete current knowledge of prices at which the transactions of all other sellers take place. The product in the narrow sense is standardized, but geographic dispersion of consumers and producers and the existence of transport costs leaves each seller with some part of his market in which he is not fully exposed to the competition of his rivals. Further, assume that entry of new firms into the industry in response to changes in profit prospects takes place only with a variable and uncertain lag. In such a market, differences in prices received

[3] "The New Sherman Act, an Instrument of Progress," *University of Chicago Law Review,* Vol. 14, No. 4 (1947), pp. 567–600.

by various sellers can persist over rather long periods, and the adjustment of prices to changes in supply or demand conditions in the market as a whole would be an uneven, time-consuming process. This situation represents, with some idealization, conditions in a number of markets in American industry.

If each seller in such a market acted independently of other sellers and tried to maximize his profits, price in the market, under given conditions, would settle at some level which might be characterized as the competitive level.[4] Could each seller sell at a higher price, up to the monopoly price, he would be better off. The aim of collusive action among sellers in such a market, therefore, would be substitution of the monopoly price for the competitive price as the ruling price in the market. This action could be achieved either through direct price fixing or through restriction of supply; for convenience the discussion will proceed in terms of price fixing. Should the monopoly price be substituted for the competitive price, any individual seller could, as is well rehearsed in elementary analysis, further improve his position by selling at a somewhat lower price, provided other sellers did not change their prices correspondingly. This shading would increase the seller's share of the market by some finite amount, limited by the imperfections and impurities of competition in the market. These same imperfections and impurities would give color to the individual seller's belief that he might succeed in shading the established price without precipitating a general and immediate reaction by all other sellers. The pursuit of such a price-shading line of action by first one, then another, seller would soon bring the market price down from the monopoly level, and ultimately, back to the competitive level.

Successful collusive action in this market would thus have two requisites:

(1) The determination of a common goal of action for all sellers: the fixing of the monopoly price, and

(2) The detection and suppression of behavior inconsistent with the achievement of the common goal: prevention of price shading. Given the character of the market, these conditions could hardly be met without a fairly voluminous stream of explicit communication among the colluding sellers. The large number of sellers, the limited information on the character of the demand for the product, the

[4] There might, in fact, be several prices, and the discussion, strictly speaking, should refer to the average level. But the simplification here adopted does not affect the essence of the argument.

complex influences of transport costs and other imperfections on the actual prices at which individual transactions are made, combine to make it extremely unlikely that the several judgments of each of the sellers as to the monopoly price should agree. Some means of comparing these judgments and adjusting them to each other would be necessary; any effective means would involve a large volume of explicit communication. Moreover, conditions in the market are not static; sellers' judgments must constantly be kept abreast of the changing market situation. This need for continuous review and revision further underlines the need for explicit communication among the colluding sellers.

But even if the first condition were somehow met, fulfillment of the second would still require some machinery of explicit communication if the collusive action of the sellers is to succeed. A method of reporting prices of all transactions so that the imperfections and impurities of the market no longer conceal the price shader is a minimum need. The communication among colluding sellers needed to insure successful price reporting may be indirect, in that it all proceeds through a trade association or statistical service, but it is none the less explicit. Further, penalties against deviation must be enforced. The fundamental penalty imposed on the price shader is the exposure of his conduct, thus opening him to the retaliation of his competitors which would deprive him of any further gain from his shading. In addition, there may be penalties – no stronger than the disapproval with which his fellows view the "chiseller" or extending to the payment of fines for departures from the concerted course of action.[5]

Thus in any market in which there are many relatively small sellers and in which there are realistic imperfections and impurities of competition, successful collusive action to fix prices (or limit supply) necessarily involves explicit communication.

What is changed in this analysis when it is applied to markets characterized by oligopoly rather than by many sellers?[6] In such markets, the chief feature of the behavior of rival sellers is the con-

[5] For an example of a system of penalty fines for sales over agreed quotas, see the account of the operations of the electric light cartel in Stocking and Watkins, *Cartels in Action,* Twentieth Century Fund (1947), pp. 304–362. See also American Linseed Oil Co. v. U.S., 262 U.S. 371 (1923), for summary of a situation in which each member of a price-fixing association deposited securities as a bond to insure compliance with the decisions of the group.

[6] No distinction need be made for the purposes of this discussion between a pure oligopolistic market, and one in which there is a competitive fringe of smaller firms. The latter are simply ignored.

scious calculation by each seller of the repercussions of his own actions on the actions of his rivals. In particular, each rival seller realizes that a price cut he initiates will be followed by his rivals, and that he cannot hope to continue to undersell his rivals by cutting his price. The significance of this recognition of mutual dependence by the rival oligopolists for the present analysis is that, given a common goal of action (condition 1 above), no machinery of reporting or enforcement is needed to secure adherence to the goal by the rivals. Each seller, knowing the common goal, realizes that he can gain nothing by actions not in conformity with it.

Although no explicit communications are required to detect and suppress deviant behavior, this in itself does not solve the problem of the definition of the common goal. The question of whether the several sellers participating in the market, exercising their judgments independently and without explicit communication among themselves (either direct or indirect), will arrive at the same (or consistent) estimates of the common goal—the monopoly price—is essentially a probability question. The greater the number of sellers making the judgment, the greater the number of variables determining the "true value" of the monopoly price, and the greater their domain of variation, the less likely it is that consistent estimates of the common goal will be formed by the several sellers acting independently. Thus it is quite likely that two firms, supplying a standard commodity with no close substitutes, in an economy in which tastes and techniques changed little and slowly, would soon discover and charge, each independently and without communication with the other, the monopoly price for their product. If the number of firms in the market is increased to ten, if demand is subject to seasonal and cyclical fluctuations, if fairly good substitutes for the product exist and others may be devised, then the probability of consistent independent judgment becomes practically zero.

The recognition of mutual dependence means that rival sellers must, in any fixed situation, charge the same price for a standard commodity; and the market would soon enforce such recognition if it were initially absent. But, in the absence of some definition of a common goal, recognition of mutual dependence alone would not insure uniformity of reaction with respect to a change in market conditions. All that could be said of a change in price, say, is that, sooner or later, the rival sellers must again sell at a uniform price; but how long the transition period endures, or how many intermediate steps occur before the price reaches its new level, would not be determined simply by the recognition by the sellers of their mutual dependence.

Consider, for example, a market in which there are three sellers of a standardized product with prices well known to all, so that price differences are impossible. At any one time, the three sellers must act uniformly with respect to price. Yet, whenever there is occasion, in the judgment of one or more sellers, for a change in price, the action of the three, in the absence of agreement on a common goal, need not be uniform. Seller A might consider it desirable to increase price by 10 per cent and initiate a change by raising his price. Seller B, however, may be reluctant to accept any change in the current price. Many patterns of reaction of B (and C) to A's increase are possible. For instance, B, being both bold and set in his judgment, may cut his price in response to A's raise; knowing that A cannot but follow him if he stands firm, and using a cut to underline his determination to resist a raise. In return, A may abandon his attempt to raise the price, or he may further undercut B, in the belief that a short period of price war will "bring B to his senses." And possible reactions of C enter in to complicate the picture further. In general, in such a situation, transitions from one price level to another might be expected to show a period of price instability before a new price level was established, rather than a single, uniform, and nearly simultaneous change by all the sellers.

However, this argument is not sufficient to prove that uniformity of action, in the sense discussed, in an oligopolistic market necessarily implies explicit communication defining a common goal of action of all the rival sellers, or in other words, that uniformity of action implies collusion in the classic sense. Given the oligopolistic character of the market, something far short of an explicit definition of the common goal can serve as a basis for such uniformity, something which may conveniently be termed "an agreement to agree." The basis of such an "agreement" is the recognition by each seller that it may be better for him to follow a single judgment of the changing market situation, even though it is not his own and he sometimes disagrees with it, than to engage in the struggle which could arise if each seller attempted to enforce his own views. Thus each seller sacrifices his exercise of independent judgment in the market; in return he gains a much greater degree of certainty as to what his rivals will do. The "agreement to agree" may result in the appearance of a single leader whose actions other sellers follow, or it may operate through a changing succession of leaders. Long continued uniformity of action, extended through a variety of situations amid changing circumstances, can therefore be taken as a basis for inferring, with a high degree of certainty, the existence of at least an "agreement to agree."[7]

Compared with the classic type of collusion and the evidence used to demonstrate it, the difficulty, or virtue, of an "agreement to agree" from the legal point of view lies in the tenuous character of the explicit communication required to establish it. Relative to the stream of explicit communication required to define and redefine continuously the common goals of action in the market, the explicit communication involved in an "agreement to agree" is almost infinitesimally small; and it certainly need never give rise to the volumes of letters, committee meetings, and so forth which constitute the classic evidences of conspiracy. Moreover, such an "agreement," once put into operation, can endure for a long period of time in changing circumstances without necessity for revision, provided only that no important new seller appears in the market. Yet some minimum meeting of minds, and some acknowledgment that such meeting has in fact occurred, is necessary to put an "agreement to agree" into operation; and therefore some finite minimum of explicit communication, at some time, is involved.

The formation and functioning of "agreements to agree" is greatly facilitated by the existence of explicit agreements which narrow the scope of independent action in the market, many of which may be of great value to the functioning of the market in other ways. Such agreements may in themselves be perfectly legal. Thus for example the uniform "extras" in steel prices, which were explicitly agreed among the producers,[8] together with the freight rate book which the American Iron and Steel Institute published, greatly facilitated the operation of price leadership under the basing point system in steel. Yet it would be very difficult for buyers to compare the offers of sellers in the steel market without uniform extras.

What guidance for the enforcement of the Sherman Act can be drawn from the preceding analysis? There can be no purely logical objection to the inclusion in the notion of collusion of "agreements to agree," and courts have tended to move along that line, as we have

[7] The uniformity of action involved is, of course, uniformity in change, not just uniformity in day to day action in a given situation. Of course, a continued lack of change over a period of widely varying cost and market conditions has the same implications as uniformity of change.

It is not inconceivable that a situation could exist in which each of a group of sellers, with the appropriate exception, trusted the judgment of one of their number better than his own, and uniformity thus would be consistent with true independence. But it is hardly likely.

[8] See TNEC, Hearings, part 19, pp. 10557–80 and 10621–35.

seen, though hardly explicitly. Thus the exhibition of parallel courses of action by rival oligopolists can legitimately form the basis of an inference of collusion in this extended sense, even if each step in the pattern is not inconsistent with the independent behavior of firms acting "competitively," that is in a rivalrous manner. Such an extension will undoubtedly make it easier for the Attorney-General to secure convictions under the Sherman Act, yet it may fail to be equally useful in providing remedies for the evils complained of. The application of the conspiracy doctrine to markets exhibiting collusion of the "classic" kind has a great pragmatic virtue. Once freed from the control of conspiracy, such markets may be expected to operate in a way consistent with the purposes underlying the Sherman Act. When the extended notion of collusion, including "agreements to agree," is applied to oligopoly situations, this virtue is lost. There may indeed be oligopolistic markets in which the elements of change and uncertainty are sufficiently dominant so that, in the absence of collusion of any sort, they may be expected to function in an "acceptable," or "workably competitive" manner. But in many oligopolistic markets, fundamental structural features of the market determine the way in which the market operates. In such cases, antitrust suits based on charges of conspiracy, and supported by evidence of parallel action, tend to draw the attention of both enforcement agencies and courts away from consideration of possible changes in the structural features of the market in which the origins of the evils complained of in the suit lie.

The result of this shift in emphasis is a preoccupation with convictions and a failure to wrestle with the difficult problem of remedies. The Tobacco case furnishes an appropriate text for this sermon. The government secured a criminal conviction against the defendant corporation which resulted in fines aggregating $312,000 being imposed on them. The fines are of course piddling as well as irrelevant; the conviction has about the same deterrent effect on the companies as would be exercised by a decree in a civil suit enjoining them to cease conspiring together. But no attempt was made to inquire into the relation of the defendants' practices to the structure of the market in such a way as to reveal meaningful possibilities of alteration. It appears dubious that any real change will occur merely as a result of the companies' efforts to avoid "crime," and the value of the government's "victory" with respect to improving competition in the cigarette market seems nil.

Thus the new willingness of the Supreme Court to find illegal conspiracy under the Sherman Act in what have been termed "agreements to agree" in oligopolistic markets, as evidenced by parallel action of rival firms, is a double-edged weapon for the enforcement agency, to be handled with the regard traditionally prescribed for such tools.

RICHARD B. HEFLEBOWER

Economics of Size*

LAST year when Lady Mehlen, executive secretary of the British Monopoly and Restrictive Practices Commission, visited Chicago, an event occurred which provides a highlight for this discussion. In explaining the work of that commission to a group of attorneys and economists assembled at the University of Chicago, Lady Mehlen emphasized that it is not as much interested in whether monopoly exists in a particular industry as in whether the effects are good or bad for the British economy. The sharp contrast between this policy and ours as expressed by Judge Learned Hand ("Congress . . . did not condone 'good trusts,' and condemn 'bad' ones; it forbade all") was pointed to by the economists present. Our antitrust policy, they stressed, is based on the presumption that no person or group of persons, public or private, is qualified to judge what is good for the economy. Only the market can make that appraisal. It is the task of antitrust policy to preserve markets in which surviving and prospering firms are those who contribute to the good of the economy. Neither a government agency nor any private group, whether a dominant corporation or a group bound together by collusion, is able to, or should be allowed to, decide what is good for the economy.

The Organizing Role of Markets

This provides the focus for our discussion, since our interest centers on large-scale enterprise *in* the market system. The private aspects of

* Reprinted from "Economics of Size" by Richard B. Heflebower in *Journal of Business,* Vol. 24 (1951), pp. 253–268, by permission of The University of Chicago Press. Copyright © 1951 by the University of Chicago.

big business are subordinate to the performance of markets made up of large-scale participants. Viewed this way, the economics of size becomes but a phase of the central problem of how economic activities shall be organized. This problem arises whenever specialization occurs and people produce more of certain goods than they sell. The activities of these specialists must be co-ordinated so that what is wanted will be produced. In a Communist society all this is done by the overhead direction of the state. Part of it may be done by the state, as Barbara Wooten pointed out during her recent visit here when she referred to the British nationalization of basic industries as an experiment in industrial organization. However, in a predominantly private property system, where government direction of production is minimal, the major economic problem is the method of achieving order in an "unplanned" economy. It does not do so by overhead direction. Rather, as businessmen and economists agree, co-ordination is achieved through the market.

Are Markets Impersonal Where Sellers Are Large?

Related to our topic, this becomes a question of whether the market system is better or worse when many or most of the sellers (or buyers) are large. This really is two questions. It is axiomatic that, when the size of the firm rises relative to the size of the market, more of the co-ordination is done by authority within firms and less relatively through exchange among firms. When a corporation integrates vertically, for example, managerial direction is substituted for one or more buying and selling steps. Likewise, when a corporation buys a competing plant, there is a reduction in horizontal co-ordination by the market and an increase in that by the authority of the firm. Viewed narrowly, is this limited area of co-ordination carried out more efficiently? That is less important than to ask whether co-ordination among the remaining autonomous enterprises is more or less effective where sellers (or buyers) become fewer and larger.

Some Opposing Views

Some economists answer these questions with a strong "Yes," for they have definite views on the adverse effects of "big business" on the economy. The conclusions of one such school stem from an analysis built on the "pure-competition" idea. By a line of reasoning, which constitutes the core of accepted economic theory, it is shown that resources would be allocated to their most appropriate and efficient use under pure competition. But such a state can obtain only when both buyers and sellers are numerous and no one buys or sells an important part of the output of a commodity. Of course few if any expect such markets to exist, particularly for industrial goods. To the degree that market structures depart from this ideal, and sellers (or buyers) become relatively larger and fewer, the markets become oligopolistic, in the economist's jargon.

Such a line of reasoning, when transferred to the policy field, leads to the conclusion that a measure of concentration, such as the percentage of a commodity sold by four firms, is a satisfactory gauge of the degree of monopoly. Consequently, a large size of firm, particularly when it means concentration, is bad per se. Followed to its ultimate policy implication, this reasoning leads to the "limitist" doctrine such as the late Professor Simons' proposal that "tentatively . . . in major industries no ownership unit should produce or control more than 5 per cent of the total output."[1]

Few economists would go this far. In particular, those who examine both the structures of industries and their actual operations under dynamic conditions reach more temperate policy conclusions. Thus Professor Clair Wilcox in his TNEC monograph includes in his "competitive" list many industries with a high degree of concentration. Indeed, Professor Clark has proposed that we be concerned with "workable competition," a concept which minimizes the structural aspects of industries and stresses those attributes which govern actual operations. Size of firm may not be the dominant influence on the market. Much of the best analysis of this sort has come from Professor E. S. Mason and his former students at Harvard, one of whom concluded that we know too little about the structure and behavior of industrial markets to have policy prescriptions with respect to them.

Others who recognize the lack of supporting evidence for a program with respect to "big business" are nonetheless insistent that a program get under way. To this end both the Committee on Cartels and Monopoly of the Twentieth Century Fund and Corwin Edwards have proposed that corporations expanding beyond a share of market or specified size be required to demonstrate that such expansion would not adversely affect competition.

It is not our purpose to judge whether policy must await definitive research or whether action is so urgently needed that it should

[1] Henry C. Simons, *A Positive Program for Laissez Faire* ("Public Policy Pamphlet," No. 15 [Chicago: University of Chicago Press, 1934]), p. 38, n. 5. . . .

be taken according to the best information available. Instead our task is to distil from the available evidence an explanation of the why and how of the large corporation and of its functioning in a competitive system.

HOW CORPORATIONS GET BIG

Relative or Absolute Size?

Already I have used the term "large corporation" and hasten to point out that there is merit in distinguishing relative size and absolute size. Both the factors which give rise to and the economic consequences of these respective size problems are potentially quite different. The economic theorist's doctrine stresses fewness of sellers or buyers of a given commodity without regard to their absolute size. Hence, if there are only two grocery stores in an isolated town, a duopoly exists. Our interest, however, is in the industrial markets; and in them fewness of sellers and large absolute size usually go together. Then there are the cases of corporate giants whose activities extend over several fields. Analysis can proceed, therefore, from relative size, which in most important cases means absolute size also, and on to the multifield industrial giants.

Growth by Building

At the root of much of the public's view, and indeed of that of the law, is the idea that giant business is an unnatural growth. Classical economics provided a rationale for such a conclusion, for it stressed the diminishing returns on management as an enterprise becomes larger and larger. Hence firms would not grow to giant size, for their inefficiency as competitors would be a check. Monopoly size could come only through some "unnatural" act, such as government grant, a merger to attain control of the market, or collusion. Such was certainly the thought of the framers of the Sherman law.

This suggests the importance of distinguishing growth by merger from growth by building. Where expansion is by building, the firm grows in the face of competition. It meets and passes market tests. To do so, it must be better than its rivals in those regards which determine success. This may be lowness of cost but not necessarily so, for in various times and places "market approval" may be earned by superior quality, progress in product development, or skill in distribution and selling. Only when success in the market stems from unfair competition can such growth be attained by uneconomic means. To engage effectively in many forms of unfair competition, a firm must have already achieved substantial size either because it has demonstrated its efficiency or because of merger.

Merger Lacks Market Tests

That last phrase carries the implication that growth by merger does not stem from a test of efficiency in the market. It is true that there are often good business reasons for mergers, and the consequences are not always uneconomic. Yet a corporation which grows by merger has not by that fact proved its greater ability in an open contest with rivals. It may be more efficient, but it has not demonstrated that in the impersonal processes of the market. Instead by one stroke a going concern is acquired and its share of the market obtained at least temporarily. We need not go so far as to assert that the merger was for market control, although many have been. Some mergers augment competition. But we can say that in and of itself growth by merger is not evidence of competitive success.

Merger a Major Source of Bigness

Unfortunately no adequate study has been made of the relative importance of growth by merger and growth by building in contributing to the present structure of American industry. The assertion is often made that most large enterprises got that way by the merger route, but no figures are presented. We do know that we have had three merger periods and that from them have emerged many of our giant corporations. There were the great mergers around the turn of the century to conform to J. Pierpont Morgan's idea of a moderated competition, but some of these mergers created monopolies in the full meaning of that word. Again during the lush twenties many combinations, not a few of which smacked of stock promotions, were thrown together. Finally, there has been a moderate boom in mergers since the last war.

This is not conclusive evidence that generally large size has been attained by merger. We know that Ford, Goodyear, and Firestone, to mention three firms involved with the automobile, grew by building. These firms' records show remarkable achievement in market tests. Of a somewhat different sort is Alcoa, whose position of dominance was first gained by a combination of patent protection and of remarkable business planning and technological and product-use advance. Then some, like Swift, expanded by building until they became large, after which growth was by both methods. Then some whose start was by merger, such as General Motors and American Can, have, since their formation, grown primarily by building. To take another situation, how does one classify Chrysler, which acquired almost bankrupt concerns and developed a giant enterprise from that uncertain base?

In spite of conflicting evidence, it is clear that a large part, indeed most, of the sizable manufacturing firms of today would be substantially smaller had their growth been by the building process only.

WHY CORPORATIONS GET BIG

Big business is not an accident; it is a product of our society and its technology. Its development has been facilitated by the corporate form of enterprise organization, permitted under our antitrust laws, and stimulated by enterpreneurial reaction to opportunities and pressures afforded by his technological and social environment. It would take a volume to do justice to such a topic. Rather than attempt to catalogue relevant factors, we shall select and highlight those which relate most closely to our major theme.

Economies of Mass Production and Size of Firm

Large-scale enterprise would not be possible without modern transportation and communication, but is giant scale required to gain the economies of mass production? It has been long recognized that the economies of large scale are substantial in much of manufacturing and distribution. From this some have jumped to the conclusion that there can be only a few sellers. That this is true in some cases is acknowledged by such supporters of limitation on the size of enterprises as Corwin Edwards and G. W. Stocking and M. W. Watkins. But, in any economy as large as ours, the volume of most products requires many sizable plants. Consequently, fewness of sellers means usually that the larger corporations are multiple-plant businesses, as is well demonstrated in a recent Federal Trade Commission analysis of census data.[2]

In examining whether there is added efficiency in having several plants under one ownership, it is usual to distinguish economies in production from those attending the scale on which purchasing, financing, and selling are carried on. Following this general approach, the above Federal Trade Commission report is built on the assumption that the former, termed "technological economies of mass production," are limited to those obtained within a particular plant.

[2] *The Divergence between Plant and Company Concentration,* 1947 (Washington, D.C., 1950).

One of the most important questions of fact about such concentration is the relation between concentration on a company basis and concentration on a plant basis. Where the two types of concentration are similar, control by large companies merely reflects a pattern of large plants and, therefore, has a technological basis. To whatever extent concentration by companies exceeds concentration by plants, the scale of business enterprise must be attributed to other circumstances than the technological economies of mass production. Where a company is large merely because its plant is large, there is no way of reducing the company's size without a fundamental change in methods of production such as probably would raise costs by reducing efficiency. Where the size of the business concern is substantially greater than that of any plant, reduction in the size of the business need alter only the central office activities, as distinguished from the technological processes, of the concern.

While the report goes on to acknowledge that "it does not attempt to determine to what extent the company concentration that is not based on large plants may be desirable or objectionable," the statement on technological requirements of scale is open to serious question. By "technological economies" more is meant than the savings in cost attributable to the size and design of machines and the physical integration of processing steps. Included also are cases in which physically separable processes can be better co-ordinated by managerial direction than through market transactions. But why must this latter type of co-ordination, that is, by management, be limited to operations located within one plant? Indeed, anyone familiar with manufacturing industries can point to numerous cases of specialization by plants within a corporate family, and specialization carried to the degree that the respective plants could not operate successfully as autonomous enterprises. In other words, such plants could not be sufficiently well integrated with other production operations through the market to be successful. For example, one can hardly visualize a regional automobile assembling plant, which may do some manufacturing, being separate in ownership from the plant where major subassemblies are put together. As another case, take the industry which the Federal Trade Commission finds to have the greatest disparity between plant and company concentration – the condensed-milk industry. There one manufacturer partially evaporates the milk at small plants located near dairy farms and then ships the output of several of these plants to a large central plant to complete the operation. One could hardly expect a market in halfway evaporated milk to develop!

Then in such problems as this economists are frequently guilty of concluding that, if one condition is changed, all others will remain the same. An error of that sort is made here, for it is assumed that single-plant companies would, in fact, build plants to the most efficient size. I suspect that, if the FTC were to continue its statistical study in another direction, it would find a close association between size of company and size of plant in the same industry. Certainly there are many cases of this sort and good reason for them. A technologically efficient plant is a very risky venture. The more efficient it is, the more specialized the equipment. The more subject, therefore, is the company to obsolescence of its investment because of technological or locational change. Such a risk can be borne only by an enterprise with diversified locations, markets, and activities.

Regardless of these important qualifications, doubt remains as to whether processing-cost advantages explain the degree of multiple-plant ownership which has developed. This is particularly true of simple-type production for local markets such as baking and ice-cream manufacture or for such national market industries as textile production. Even in national-market, more-intricate-processing industries there is doubt as to whether processing-cost advantages *alone* explain the modern industrial giant. If important economic advantages do accrue in such cases, they must be in other phases of the business operation. Most large manufacturing firms would be substantially smaller were their size not to exceed that necessary for processing efficiency alone.

In searching for other causal forces, one can extend the technological to encompass both the technical know-how of a managerial group and research. There is much to the contention that such services are purchasable. There are management and engineering firms whose services are for hire. Yet large concerns often have what amounts to inside engineering consultants or an advisory group whose services are available to operating divisions. This is even more true of research. It seems unlikely that outside research will focus on the peculiar problems of a firm in the fashion that a management-built and management-directed group will.

In both these cases an appraisal must stem from the decisions of business. These services can be hired or "owned." Since no one of them has any important bearing on whether the firm can exercise market control, it would seem the preference to have "inside" services of these types indicates the general superiority of that arrangement, and, since large concerns appear to make relatively more use of such specialized services, this suggests that they contribute to efficiency.

Distribution Problems and Company Size

From production we turn to the field of selling in which the advantages of size are more nebulous and the decision often reflects one's view of economic processes. To those who idealize pure competition, all sales effort is uneconomic and exploitive. Goods should sell themselves. Few take such an extreme view. A more moderate conception, and one which I suspect is back of the thinking of some proponents of extreme action in the antitrust field, is that manufacturers should sell to general-type wholesalers or retailers. There is no need, according to this view, for a manufacturer to have a distribution program. He does not need specialty wholesale or retail outlets. Instead all distribution should be similar to that for dry groceries and general hardware.

But if one holds, as I do, that there is some valid economic explanation for market processes as they have developed, he will see that the seller has reason to be concerned about distribution problems. He does have a sales problem, and that, according to the type of goods he produces, requires a program. One facet of this may be that he requires a field sales force. He may need to do his own wholesaling, and often he needs a line of products which together make a market family. These developments all occur without any notable degree of, or objective of, market control. Even small firms have such programs, but one must acknowledge that success in such a program does bring a degree of control in the sense that the seller is better able to avert unfavorable developments, such as the loss of an outlet, or to seize favorable opportunities. So selling effort may be designed to overcome the imperfections of market, but, in so doing, it makes the markets more imperfect for competing sellers.

Vertical Integration: A Move to Offset the Imperfections of, or to Control, Markets?

A similar confusion of cause and effect can exist with respect to vertical integration. A manufacturer may undertake his own wholesaling as part of a program of getting wider, and perhaps lower-cost distribution and consumer acceptance. He may have found that independent wholesalers do not push his goods with dealers and consumers or that they are slow to adopt new merchandising techniques. In other words, the markets are not working well from his viewpoint and perhaps from that of the economy also. But success in doing his own wholesaling and branding carries an element of control, whether intentional or not. For example, the manufacturer who undertakes his own distribution because of a fear that an independent wholesaler might drop his line and leave him unrepresented in an area is not willing to let that representation rest on market decision; he wants to control it. That does not necessarily have an adverse effect on market-wide competition; competition among factory brands of various manufacturers may be avid.

The contrast we are stressing here stands out even more clearly when a company integrates backward. That may be done to offset poor quality or irregular supplies or to offset monopoly at earlier levels. There are clear cases in which supplying markets are not working well. It may be, as is often possible, that vertical steps can be better integrated through management than through the market. That seems to be true in A. and P.'s manufacturing operations.[3] Indeed, much of the success of chain stores stems from integrating the wholesaling and retailing functions.

Backward integration can also bring control. That, to use A. and P. again, is what has been asserted about some local buying by its produce-buying subsidiary. To be effective, however, the integrated concern must be so large a share of the market at some stage that it substantially reduces the sale alternatives of its suppliers.

Finance and Managerial Incentives

For the large corporation the means of expansion are usually at hand. While much has been made of the fact that large concerns retain a lesser share of earnings than do smaller ones, the fact remains that one of the former may retain millions in a year. This, added to funds currently coming from depreciation charges, makes enough available in one year to enable the large firm to enter most lines of business on a substantial scale. Where external funds are desired, they are available on favorable terms, as our postwar experience shows.

This means in part that a large concern becomes to a degree an investment trust. Its activities are so diversified that its earnings and prospects mean the earnings and prospects of a type of business. Whether aware of that or not, investors, when buying stock or passively letting earnings be retained, take that view.

Retained earnings leads us to the subject of who makes the investment decisions. Certainly in classical economics it was assumed that the owner did. For corporate finance this would mean that the common stockholders would pass on the use of retained earnings. Funds from outside would come only after a market test had been met; that

[3] See M. A. Adelman, "The A & P Case: A Study of Applied Economic Theory," *Quarterly Journal of Economics,* LXIII (May, 1949), 246–47. See also Boris Emmet and John E. Jeuck, *Catalogues and Counters* (Chicago: University of Chicago Press, 1950), pp. 404 ff., with respect to Sears Roebuck's manufacturing and its relations with suppliers.

is, when investors were satisfied with the prospects. In the modern corporation in operation things are quite different. The directors determine the earnings to be withheld and the use to be made of those and other internal funds. While directors presumably are elected, they are, in the typical case, elected by the proxies voted by members of the management-director group. In many corporations a large share, and in some a majority, of the directors are also active officers.

This is not the place to appraise the full consequences of the so-called divorcement of ownership and control. Our interest is in its effect on size. Is the management in a position to decide upon the internal funds to be available? Is it also free, in fact, to decide upon how they shall be used? Both questions are answered affirmatively but within limits, for stockholders may rebel or the performance of the price of the corporation's stock may signal a market reaction. These are wide limits, so we go on. Will management be inclined to expand without careful study of prospects? Does the desire for the prestige which goes with size outweigh caution? The answers to these latter questions are not known and may not be knowable.

The possibility of "growthitis" cannot be ruled out. Certainly industry asserts that government agencies and labor unions have that ailment. Why not corporations also? The motives of prestige for corporate leaders, and their feeling of power, are there. With the passivity of stockholders business leaders are not under narrow-range restraint in their decisions. Does the potential activation of stockholders or the standards of success or other mores of the business community restrain decision-makers from pressing for growth for growth's sake? It is possible that the answers to such queries are affirmative, but I have not seen evidence which would make such an answer definitive.

Taxation and Big-Company Expansion

No discussion of this sort is complete without a reference to taxation. I shall mention only the points which fit the general plan of my argument. In spite of the double taxation of corporate earnings, the corporate tax, combined with the capital gains tax, encourages expansion by existing enterprises. This is true of corporations of all sizes and may even be most true of the small one in which the owners hope to minimize their personal taxes and recoup via a capital gain at a later date. Then, at that later date, the firm is ripe for "'mergeritis" as the aging founders seek to cash in on the growth of their enterprise.

The incremental character of the personal income tax encourages people to invest in large corporations. Small concerns, if successful, offer the chance of much greater earnings, but that is only a chance. If successful, much of the differential gain is taken by incremental taxes. If failure occurs, the loss can be taken only against capital gains. Four per cent certain is better than 9 per cent possible. The devil himself could not have devised a better urge toward growth by established large firms rather than by new ventures than that provided by our present tax system.

Influence of Organized Labor and of Government Controls

Any analysis of the reasons for the growth of big business would be incomplete without reference to the influence of government controls and of organized labor. Both influences give, on occasion, some real opportunity for small business. In part this stems from conscious preferential rules or acts. In part also it comes from preferential enforcement of union rules and public regulations. In part also this stems from the "holes" in all regulatory procedures, public and private, and small enterprise is better adapted to finding and taking advantage of such imperfect coverage of controls or rules.

On balance, though, it seems that these new labor market and governmental controls, while not favoring large business directly, nevertheless press for larger and larger business units. A major organized labor policy is to wipe out interarea and interplant wage differentials, while pressing the level of wages up toward what the most efficient can pay. Wage differentials often represented differences in efficiency, which in turn stemmed from differences in degree of mechanization. When large labor-input firms' wages advance relatively, they must sell out or mechanize. Either tends to bring larger corporations and fewer sellers. In some cases firms find it necessary to buy out suppliers in order to control labor negotiations in those plants and keep the material flow going. None of these aspects of dealing with organized labor influences firm size as much as does the mere task of negotiation and administration of a labor agreement. This calls for a specialized staff which only a substantial firm can afford. . . . Organized labor, I suspect, is one more of the evolutionary influences from which is emerging the good-sized, but perhaps not the giant, firm.

In much the same way, the problems of dealing with government call for some of the same specialization. This is certainly true of the federal government as a buyer. But I am thinking more of the multifarious quasi- or fully regulatory activities which become a substantial cost in time and money to business. As such, this may be one more consequence – I do not insist on the word "price" – of the social trends of our era.

Merger to Reduce Competition

Brief reference should be made to two other topics in this incomplete cataloguing of forces behind the growth of big business. One is promotional profits, and we shall pass over it with this mere mention. The other is merger for control. Between 1875 and 1910 such was the announced object of many mergers. Most moves in that direction have been more cautious and piecemeal since the antitrust laws have been administered with more vigor. Indeed, Professor Stigler refers to the recent ones as "merger for oligopoly,"[4] the economists' term for "fewness of sellers." By this he meant that modern mergers do not place a high percentage of the output of a commodity in the hands of one company. Instead a few large sellers emerged, as in the copper industry. In most of these cases, I suspect that the minds of those engineering these mergers were on what they would term "business objectives." Among these are strengthening a firm's position in a section of the market, widening the line to offer dealers, acquiring patents owned by the merged concerns, etc. But each such merger may also have had the effect of weakening rivals, making entry more difficult, tying dealers to the now enlarged concern, etc. Whatever reduces the alternatives of participants in the market reduces competition. What to the seller is "strengthening his market position" may mean "weakening of competition." Even more important is the question as to whether and by what means giant rivals dare compete. This is a topic to which we shall return.

THE GIANT, MULTIPRODUCT CORPORATION

A phenomenon of recent significance is the giant corporation whose activities spread over many fields. Usually, but not necessarily, these companies sell a substantial share of the output in one or more commodity fields. They are, as was indicated earlier, somewhat like investment trusts for a commodity area. As such their most obvious characteristic is their giant size and their multi-product operations. Other less obvious, but perhaps as important, attributes will be brought out as we explain how they got the way they are.

[4] G. J. Stigler, "Monopoly and Oligopoly by Merger," *American Economic Review*, XL, No. 2 (1950), 31–32.

Management Financial Corporations

Both the absolute size and the spreadeagle character of the business of these firms need to be explained. All that I have said before about influences for growth, except the size needed for efficiency in processing, is relevant here. Indeed, some of these influences are accentuated, such as availability of funds. These corporations are typically the blue chips, and their stocks rate as investments. They can borrow on terms comparable to those of governments.

Indeed, I suggest that these corporations can best be viewed as "management financial corporations." This term departs from two connotations of "investment trust." One departure is that their role in initiating new fields of production and sale is more important than mere investment in stock of going concerns. Such corporations have become a major source of new product and process advance in this complex economy of ours. The second is that the managements of these giants actively participate in the policies of the operating divisions or subsidiaries. Top management really becomes an "activated board of directors," a fact recognized formally at Du Pont, where the two policy-making committees are board committees. Then these giants are financial corporations in two senses. One is that control over finance is never decentralized within the corporation; in fact, finance is the chief device for controlling operations. Second, the corporation serves as a pool of funds for the operating divisions. The vast inside funds available each year plus the ease of acquiring funds outside makes this possible. The operating divisions have to sell their needs not to a group of bankers but to an informed entrepreneurial group, top management. Finally, these giants are also pools of managerial skill. Operating divisions can draw on the nation's best, but inside, management counselors; top-grade management of a versatile sort is available for any new ventures the corporation may initiate.

Giants Become Multiproduct Concerns

The diversification of activities of these giant corporations reflects in varying degree public policy, conscious managerial policy, and opportunities. There can be no doubt that, consciously or unconsciously, managements seek to avoid acquiring too large a share of particular commodity markets because of fear of antitrust attack.

Here and there one also finds an inkling of two more constructive reasons. There seems to be a perception of the fact that, if competition does not continue virile, the corporation's operating divisions will become decadent. The pressure of outside competition is a greater cause of efficiency and progress than overhead direction, whether private or public, can be. Second, there is a realization that established commodity fields offer less opportunity in earnings, in prestige, and in "fun" than do developing areas. Often these giants' share declines in the old, basic commodity field in which they first became great, while they do their share or more of the pioneering. Some of this stems from their research operations. Other cases come from half-developed ideas which they buy, or their staff detects old areas of production ripe for a redoing. Consequently, such firms tend to spread out from their original production and sales fields in directions of promising profit margins. Old lines which settle into staid methods and earnings, while rarely sloughed off, are not expanded; so these companies become, from the stockholders' viewpoint, an open-end investment trust.

Management Decentralization and Its Effects

Such size and diversification of activities force a decentralization of management. In general, the pattern of this decentralization is to give to operating divisions most of the advantages without some of the disadvantages of an autonomous business. To succeed, divisional management must have discretion over those activities which determine profit or loss for the division. At the same time the division's freedom may be restrained with respect to anything on which the corporation must present a common front, such as public and labor relations. The division management is relieved of those worries which can be assumed by central management but which would hamper an autonomous venture. One such item is always finance. On other occasions it may be raw-material purchase or wholesale distribution.

From this decentralization two results emerge. One is that the crimping effects of size on managerial efficiency are minimized or averted. Second, giant corporations' stake in virile competition is high, for their management-efficiency scheme of decentralization will work only as long as each of the product markets in which they sell is actively competitive. This is because the success of decentralization is in permitting operating personnel to meet the opportunities and restraints of their product markets in order to earn as good a departmental profit-and-loss statement as possible.

THE EFFICIENCY OF LARGE ENTERPRISE

At several points in our exploration into the reasons for giant enterprises we have raised the question of economic efficiency. Before we bring those questions together, we must inquire as to what is meant by efficiency. Obviously it is not a synonym for private advantage, for we are concerned with advantage to the economy. Economic efficiency to some, particularly those who look at these problems through pure-competition glasses, means lowness of cost or, more specifically, of production cost. Were that an adequate test, it would be difficult to apply it, for no set of figures is more tricky than is product costs. No comprehensive, reliable study of this sort has been made. But does efficiency consist solely of production costs? To answer affirmatively is to assume that technological progress and product acceptance and distribution take care of themselves. These are patently incorrect assumptions; social efficiency is the efficiency of the whole business process required by actual problems of getting goods people want produced and in their hands.

When we raise (in this more accurate context) the question of how to test efficiency, we find that it is the net result of the cost and effectiveness with which several activities of varying importance among industries or in the same industry at various times are performed. Most of these aspects of efficiency cannot be quantified. How, then, can we reach judgments?

Perhaps something can be inferred from whether firms of widely varying size exist in the same industry. If they do, Professor A. R. Burns would conclude that the economies of scale are not significant.[5] But this is far from an adequate explanation and is often incorrect. If one examines firms of markedly different size in the same industry, he will find that they really are not in the same business. Their product lines differ in variety; they have different-sized markets geographically; they use different channels of sale and appeal to different buying motives. Hence, were it possible to find a common denominator by which to compare these firms, all we would have is a measure of the size appropriate to engaging in various phases of a loosely defined industry.

If in desperation we were to fall back on profits as a test of efficiency, we would be no better off, for then we could be accused of circular reasoning. The main concern about big business is the possibility that it may have monopoly power. Certainly, if it did, that would be reflected in its earnings. So using earnings as a test of efficiency would assume that large and small firms were equally competitive. We do not know whether they are; that is what we are trying to find out.

[5] *The Decline of Competition* (New York: McGraw-Hill Book Co., 1936), p. 431.

What we come to, then, is that efficiency must be judged qualitatively. To do that precisely would require exhaustive study of each industry. Only a few such studies have been made. On more general grounds, our whole line of reasoning establishes a presumption in favor of efficiency being reflected in the size of firms which have grown by building. That does not help in the numerous instances of large concerns which have grown by merger, for, while that method of growth is not prima facie evidence of inefficiency, it does not establish efficiency either. This is as far as we can go; any broad generalization is a speculation.

COMPETITION AND SIZE

Big business is here to stay, for it is both caused by and has become part of the technology and social framework of our era. This is not to say that all the corporate size that has developed is good or inevitable. Had the recent amendment to Section 7 of the Clayton Act been on the books since 1914 and been aggressively enforced, many corporations would be substantially smaller today, without social loss. Rather this is a forecast that, while here and there a disintegration may occur by failure or court order, the face of Industrial America will not be altered noticeably thereby. The basic question is whether competition is "workable" with the degree of giantism we have and will build through the growth, not the merger, route in the future.

The answer, we shall find, depends on one's view of how the competitive processes work and on what one wants competition to do. Both of these have been widely heralded by economists and lawyers as depending on "concentration." . . .

"Concentration" is a slippery term for two reasons. While it refers to the share of a market in few hands, the concept of product or commodity is vague. Generally the industry classifications of the census are adopted, but those were developed for other reasons. Hence closely substitutable lard and shortening are in separate industries, although it happens that treating them as one would not change the concentration radically. It does, however, make a great difference whether virgin and scrap aluminum are considered as one or as two industries.

Second, what does the idea of concentration tell you about the size distribution of sellers? Many patterns are possible. There may be one large seller and several small ones, as in aluminum, virgin and scrap together. There may be a few large ones and several small producers, as is the case in tires. The size distribution may start with one sizable firm and taper over quite a distance, as in steel. Or there may be for practical purposes just a handful of sellers, as in cigarettes.

While such measurement problems call for caution in use of data, it is possible to answer the question, "Has concentration increased?" It is popular to say that it has, but calm research does not support that view. Professor M. A. Adelman, in an unpublished manuscript, has critically reviewed the data and produced a number of new and ingenious compilations. Among the major findings is that instead of the 1932 forecast of Berle and Means, that a sharp increase in the share of corporate wealth in the hands of a group of top-size corporations would occur, the proportion has fallen. While concentration within some industries has increased since 1937, as shown by share of output of the four largest sellers, it has fallen in others; for the economy as a whole no major change has occurred.

Aside from the change or lack of change in concentration, what is it beyond an interesting statistic? To some it is an index of monopoly, and that is the end of the argument. Such a conclusion could be reached from some of the work of economic theorists referred to above, and sometimes the economists fall for this conclusion. Suppose, however, a man from Mars had been indoctrinated with these connotations of concentration and the statistics of American industry and had then had a chance to observe the American economy in operation. What a shock he would have! Instead of widespread monopoly profits, idle facilities, and technological stagnation — all the supposed consequences of monopoly — he would find the opposite. Yet I fear that some college students have a similar surprise in store for them when they leave the classroom and become familiar with the economy in operation.

Concentration is only one, and perhaps not the most important, fact to know about an industry if one is to appraise its competitiveness. The concentration idea is part of a schema which includes a number of assumptions, which may or may not be applicable in particular industries. Among these assumptions are that the sellers are alike, that their product is standardized and is so judged by buyers, and that these firms are fully informed of the future.

These facts are true only to varying degrees, if at all, in particular industries. Once one recognizes that, does that mean that competition will be more or less virile under these realistic conditions?

In part the answer depends on what one means by competition. To some the only effective and beneficial form of competition is a contest over price. That is, sales ought to be gained by offering the lowest price. Ideally, according to this view all transactions should be on auctions. Indeed, the usual inference is that if competition takes other than the price form, particularly if competition is sales effort, that is prima facie evidence of impure competition.

In part also the answer depends on what one means by price. Far too much economic analysis continues to be carried on in terms of "quoted" prices rather than "transaction" prices. Then, the presence or absence of significant labor and material price movements does much more to explain real price changes than does concentration in the industry. Beyond this the sellers' "mix" of long and short margin items can vary receipts relative to cost even under fixed price schedules as we learned so well during the war.

But my major contention is that in most industrial areas competition is among sellers who offer unlike goods. Recall that I pointed to the coexistence of firms of widely divergent size as being explained by the fact that they are not in the same business. Instead what they sell, how they sell, and to whom they sell, and with what attendant services varies significantly in most cases. Consequently, competitors do not hit head-on. They try to go around each other, to blunt the impact of rivals, etc. We have heterogeneous competition, a fact which creates the maze of items, channels of distribution, sale terms, and sales appeals which are the modern market. From this comes competition as it is, in which close substitutes are available, so that rarely does a seller have enough isolation that he can get a noncompetitive price.

By such indirect devices each seller tries to avert the consequences of a direct open price cut but, in doing so, pulls the level of realization toward cost. Inexorably, with some interferences, and perhaps tardily, what and how much is produced, how it is sold, and what is realized for it are pulled in the directions warranted by conditions of cost and demand. There are exceptions of course, but there is little evidence that the exceptions are correlated with bigness.

It is only when the man from Mars, or the student from the classroom, sees competition in this fashion that he can resolve the apparent inconsistency between industrial concentration and market results which could come only from active competition. Such competition may not be ideal, but it is real.

There remains the question of what one wants competition to do. If he insists that only direct price competition can bring correct adjustments, I have no patience with him, for he has an astigmatic view of the economic process. If he feels that prompt adjustment is needed, he will be disappointed, for the processes to which I allude work more slowly than does an auction market. This can be a matter of great concern; that is, it is if one feels that the solutions to such great problems as economic stability rest on prompt adjustment in the commodity markets. Such was the view of those who initiated the "price rigidity" conflict of the 1930's when industry was accused of lengthening the depression by not pricing as did agriculture. Progressively, however, economists are coming to view that problem in a different way. Economic stability stems primarly from the movement of such aggregates as consumer incomes and the saving or spending of that income and the decisions to invest. Such is the Keynesian argument. From it comes the idea that commodity markets need not adjust so quickly; indeed, there is some merit in a degree of stability. So that alleged radical, Keynes, provides a rationale for the workability of competition in an economy of large business units!

From the preceding analysis comes the conclusion that competition can be, and often has been, effective where sellers are few and large. But such conclusions must not become blinders. There are also degrees of size which can be dangerous either by themselves or because they facilitate effective tacit collusion. Whether or not size is dangerous depends on how well the market restrains the large seller from exerting power and prods it to be efficient. Judgments on that depend on a number of variables, of which size itself is but one, and often not the controlling one.

While the conditions for effective competition cannot be easily generalized, we can agree on one basic standard. If size, even the size for maximum efficiency, threatens competition, a choice must be made. On that I have no trouble; competition comes first. The market system must not be weakened in performing its task of guiding economic affairs. Therefore we can pass over the question of how big firms must be to be efficient. Certainly the ambition of particular firms must be subsidiary. We can afford somewhat less rapid progress, or whatever price of that sort we have to pay, for maintaining effective competition.

All this does not support those views that effective competition can be judged by mere statistics of firm size and numbers of sellers. Such views of competition show either naïveté or intellectual laziness. Finding the real substance of competition requires hard, grubbing work.

Our understanding of the essential conditions of competition can be advanced only by firsthand study of a variety of markets. To do this well requires firsthand facts of the sort usually termed "confidential." Here is where business itself comes in. Only with its cooperation in supplying to analysts the essential information about market operations can the major issue in the economics of size be resolved; that is, how much size is consistent with workable competition.

CONCLUSION

The papers presented here reflect the extent of disagreement on what antitrust decisions mean. Although there is some agreement among the authors, notably on the relevance of economic analysis, on the increasing importance of the *per se* doctrine, and on the flexibility of the rule of reason, there is no consensus on the relevant criteria for determining future policy. With the exception of Oppenheim, and possibly Heflebower, there is basic agreement that the antitrust laws, if anything, need to be strengthened. Oppenheim would dilute much of antitrust by specific incorporation in it of the concept of workable competition which Adams finds to be a rather meaningless one.

Stressing the role of even unexerted power as the criterion of what is prohibited, Rostow's view is rather close to Kaysen's implied emphasis on structure. But while Rostow thinks that power is and should be the crux, Kaysen considers structural variables important but neglected factors. Kahn would not be pinned down on any criterion as the operative one, but nonetheless tends to emphasize, more than others, the leading role of intent.

The above articles are atypical of antitrust literature in general in their relevance and insight. But they are typical in their varying interpretations of what is and what should be. This clashing of opinions might be regarded as symptomatic of the ineffectuality of antitrust policy, of its impenetrable anarchy, of its vacillation. To be sure, there is an element of truth in this view. But these features are also a testament to its sensitivity and ability to adjust to the changing economic realities of a dynamic world. This is a characteristic of all viable constitutions. In a real sense, the antitrust statutes are our Economic Constitution.

operation. In seeking to analyze the essentially [illegible]
[illegible]
[illegible] with workable competition.

CONCLUSION

The papers presented here reflect the extent of disagreement on what antitrust decisions mean. Although there is some agreement among the authors, notably on the relevance of economic analysis, on the increasing importance of the per se doctrine, and on the feasibility of the rule of reason, there is no consensus on the relevant criteria for determining future policy. With the exception of Oppenheim, and possibly Hale-power, there is basic agreement that the antitrust laws, if anything, need to be strengthened. Oppenheim would dilute much of antitrust by specific incorporation in it of the concept of workable competition which Adams finds to be a rather meaningless one.

Stressing the role of even unexerted power as the criterion of what is prohibited, Rostow's view is rather close to Kaysen's implied emphasis on structure. But while Rostow thinks that power is and should be the crux, Kaysen considers structural variables important but neglected factors. Dirlam would not be pinned down on any criterion as the operative one, but nonetheless tends to emphasize, more than others, the leading role of intent.

The above articles are atypical of antitrust literature in general in their relevance and insight. But they are typical in their varying interpretations of what is and what should be. This clashing of opinions might be regarded as symptomatic of the ineffectuality of antitrust policy, of its unmanageable quality, of its vacillation. To be sure, there is an element of truth in this view. But these features are also testament to the complexity and difficulty of coping with the changing economic realities of a dynamic world. They are characteristic of all viable institutions and, in a real sense, the antitrust laws are an economic Constitution.

SUGGESTIONS FOR READING

The basic article on the origins of the Sherman Act is W. Letwin's "Congress and the Sherman Antitrust Law: 1887–1890," *University of Chicago Law Review,* Volume 23 (1956) p. 221. An interesting review and analysis of public opinion as manifested in newspapers and periodicals of the time is found in S. D. Gordon, "Attitudes Towards Trusts Prior to the Sherman Act," *Southern Economic Journal,* Volume 30 (1963) p. 156. The most comprehensive treatment is H. B. Thorelli, *The Federal Antitrust Policy: Origination of an American Tradition* (London, 1954).

A most useful guide to interpreting the antitrust laws is the *Report* of The Attorney General's National Committee To Study The Antitrust Laws (Washington, 1955). A bitter comment on the genesis and operation of the Committee is the article by L. B. Schwartz, a member, "Committees, Politics, Scholarship and Law Reform: Antitrust Studies in Perspective," *University of Pennsylvania Law Review,* Volume 104 (1955) p. 153. For a contrary view see S. N. Barnes, "Background and Report of the Attorney General's Committee," *loc. cit.*, p. 147.

Cogent and comprehensive discussions of antitrust standards will be found in C. D. Edwards, "Public Policy and Business Size," *Journal of Business,* Volume 24 (1951) p. 280; A. E. Kahn, "Standards for Antitrust Policy," *Harvard Law Review,* Volume 67 (1953) p. 28; M. Handler, *Antitrust in Perspective* (New York, 1957). An excellent and sympathetic evaluation of the evolution and meaning of antitrust is J. P. Miller, "Antitrust Policy: The United States Experience," in *Competition, Cartels, and Their Regulation,* ed. Miller (Amsterdam, 1962).

A relatively early and powerful argument for a structuralist approach is W. S. Bowman, "Toward Less Monopoly," *University of Pennsylvania Law Review,* Volume 101 (1953) page 589. Wary of the effects of government interference, Bowman argues for the establishment of an acceptably competitive structure and a subsequent hands-off policy. A similar and more extreme structuralist remedy, though for different reasons, is advocated by L. B. Schwartz, "New Approaches to the Control of Oligopoly," *University of Pennsylvania Law Review,* Volume 109 (1960) p. 31. The most comprehensive and judicious treatment of this approach is D. F. Turner and C. Kaysen, *Antitrust Policy: An Economic and Legal Analysis* (Cambridge, Mass., 1959). The opposition to this approach, and the argument that there is no inherent relationship between size and performance, is perhaps best put by M. Adelman in "Effective Competition and the Antitrust Laws," *Harvard Law Review,* Volume 61 (1948), p. 1289, and in "Integration and Antitrust Policy," *op. cit.,* Volume 63 (1949), p. 27. Performance as the standard is critically evalued and attacked by C. D. Edwards, "Use and Abuse of Economics in Antitrust Litigation," American Bar Association, *Antitrust Law Section,* Volume 20 (1962), p. 38.

An excellent summary discussion of market concepts and their use in Sherman and Clayton Act litigation is G. R. Hall, "Market Definition and Antitrust Policy," *Washington and Lee Law Review,* Volume 20 (1963), page 47. In "A Critique of Concepts of Workable Competition," *Quarterly Journal of Economics,* Volume 72, (1958), p. 380, S. H. Sosnick reviews and compares the published views on workable competition of eighteen economists. A comprehensive argument for workable competition as the standard is J. M. Clark, *Competition as a Dynamic Process* (Washington, 1961). For a critical review see K. E. Boulding in the *Annals* of The American Academy of Political and Social Science, Volume 343 (1962), p. 181. J. Weissman in "Is Oligopoly Illegal: A Jurisprudential Approach," *Quarterly Journal of Economics,* Volume 74 (1960), p. 437, argues one should not even try to enforce competition in an oligopoly situation. A somewhat similar view, critical of even workable competition as too stringent, is held by C. E. Griffin in "A Realistic Antitrust Policy," *Harvard Business Review,* Volume 34 (1956), p. 76, which is a vulgarization of the Schumpeterian thesis. A somewhat similar idea, based on the desirability of certain kinds of joint action, termed "interfirm organization," is found in A. Phillips, *Market Structure, Organization and Performance* (Harvard, 1962). This is essentially a plea for legalizing some forms of collusion. A similar but more explicit and forward argument is presented in B. Smith, "Effective Competition: Hypothesis for Modernizing the Antitrust Laws," *New York University Law Review,* Volume 26 (1951), p. 405. The ultimate of this line of argument, that there is hardly any monopoly and oligopoly in the U. S., and what there is costs almost nothing in welfare loss as a result of misallocation, is to be found in D. Schwartzman, "The Economics of Antitrust Policy," *Antitrust Bulletin,* Volume 6 (1961), p. 235. For a very strong attack on the above line of argument, holding that economic analysis, and the concept of workable competition, is often used as a rationalization for the dilution of the laws and their ineffectual enforcement, see G. W. Stocking, "Economic Change and The Sherman Act: Some Reflections on Workable Competition," *University of Virginia Law Review,* Volume 44, (1958), p. 537.

Chapter 1, "The Judicial Architects of the Rule of Reason," in Handler, *Antitrust in Perspective,* his "Some Unresolved Problems of Antitrust," *University of Columbia Law Review,* Volume 62, (1962),

p. 930, and L. Loevinger, "Rule of Reason in Antitrust Law," *University of Virginia Law Review,* Volume 50 (1964), p. 23, are all interesting and important interpretations, from two different points of view, of the development and function of the rule of reason.

The literature on the effectiveness of antitrust policy is vast. The interesting view that antitrust has been "effective" because it has not been militantly enforced, putting the blame for unemployment and other economic ills on what antitrust there has been, is held by T. J. Kreps, "An Evaluation of Antitrust Policy; Its Relation To Economic Growth, Full Employment, and Prices," Study Paper No. 22, Joint Economic Committee, Congress of the United States, 86th Congress, 2d Session (Washington: 1960). A very much contrary view, that the laws are good, dynamic, and effective is presented by V. R. Hansen, "Antitrust Laws in a Changing Economy," *University of California Law Review,* Volume 6 (1959), p. 183. For an even more laudatory view see B. J. Rashid, "What is Right With Antitrust?", *Antitrust Bulletin,* Volume 5 (1960), p. 5. It should be mentioned that at that time Rashid was Chief of the Trial Section, Antitrust Division. Representative current views can be found in the "Symposium" in the *Journal of the American Bar Association,* Volume 23 (1963). A somewhat earlier but still important set of views is presented in D. M. Keezer, ed., "The Effectiveness of the Federal Antitrust Laws: A Symposium," *American Economic Review,* Volume 39, Supplement (1949), p. 689. A completely different opinion, denigrating the effectiveness as well as the concept of antitrust and calling for government planning, is most ably put by M. D. Reagan in his *The Managed Economy* (New York, 1963).

The student of economics interested in the merging of law and economics in the courtroom during actual litigation is referred to M. S. Massel, *Competition and Monopoly, Legal and Economic Issues,* (Washington, 1962). This is an excellent, comprehensive, and clear presentation of how economics is used in the preparation and presentation of antitrust cases. A shorter, less comprehensive, more specifically legal procedure oriented set of readings is found in "Trial of an Antitrust Action: A Symposium," American Bar Association, *Section on Antitrust Law,* Volume 18, (1961), p. 13. The contributions are by outstanding practitioners and legal scholars, such as Handler, Freund, Dixon, and Loevinger.

For a comprehensive historical introduction to the interplay of legal and economic factors, *Monopoly in Economics and the Law* by Donald Dewey (Chicago, 1959) is recommended.